A Forgotten Revival

Recollections of the great Revivals of East Anglia and North East Scotland of 1921

Stanley C Griffin

Day One

© Day One Publications 2000
First printed 1992

Scripture quotations are from The Authorized Version.

British Library Cataloguing in Publication Data available
ISBN 1 903087 06-6

Published by Day One Publications
3 Epsom Business Park, Kiln Lane, Epsom, Surrey KT17 1JF.
01372 728 300 **FAX** 01372 722 400
email—sales@dayone.co.uk
www.dayone.co.uk

Designed by Steve Devane and printed by Clifford Frost Wimbledon SW19 2SE

Dedication

To the memory of my mother.
As a young woman she saw her
prayers answered when her future
husband, my father, was among the
first wave of converts in the revival.
She prayed for me until I was
converted and continued until she was
called home.

Contents

Acknowledgements

Many friends have shared with me their experience of the revival and their personal reminiscences. Some have since gone to 'be with Christ'; some are mentioned in the book.

The present minister of London Road Baptist Church Lowestoft, Trevor Edworthy, loaned me over fifty press cuttings which were carefully collected at the time by a member of the church.

Without the help of Pamela Stacey, a member of my local church and Rev Brian Edwards, this work would not have been completed. Pamela spent many hours editing and word-processing my original typescript. Brian encouraged me to persevere, gave me the benefit of his knowledge and experience, wrote the foreword and did the final editing.

Pastor John Woods and the members of Beresford Road Evangelical Church, have constantly urged me on and have prayed for each stage of the preparation of this book.

Finally, I thank my wife Joy who sat quietly by me and encouraged me through many long evenings.

From its first publication in 1992 it was encouraging to see *A Forgotten Revival* go into a second printing. But it is even more encouraging to know that in this new edition we have the result of Stanley Griffin's continued research. So, with new material and additional illustrations, we now have a fuller account of the revival that began in Lowestoft in 1921. For those who, through this book, will be introduced to the revival, it will be worth me repeating what I wrote in the first edition about this 'Forgotten revival'.

From one point of view it is hardly surprising that a revival in Lowestoft should have been forgotten. The wild and beautiful East Anglian coast, together with its rich agricultural hinterland, is not one of the best known corners of England. The coastal town of Lowestoft is known by many today only for its dwindling fishing fleet and a theme park. But the work of God that began in Lowestoft in 1921 and then spread rapidly across East Anglia and into northeast Scotland, should not have been overlooked by evangelical Christians for so long. It was, after all, the last widespread revival in England. I love the coast of East Anglia and have spent many holidays there. The fact that my father was born at Caister where my grandfather was a coast guard, and that my parents returned to Suffolk on retirement, all added to my natural interest in the area. I have East Anglian blood in my veins! I first discovered accounts of the revival in Lowestoft whilst I was researching for my own book on revival in the 1980s. At first I was frustrated by the almost complete absence of published material relating to this great work of God. Articles and cuttings were available only to those who had both time and ability to ferret them out. Then I met Stanley Griffin and discovered that for years he had been quietly and patiently combining his daily work with diligent research into the Lowestoft revival. It was crucial that his work should be published for the benefit of all who are concerned with the subject of spiritual revival.

Stanley Griffin has written a carefully researched account of a revival, not from a dry academic perspective, but with his own heart on fire with the hope that God will come again to this nation. His scriptural analysis of the revival and its aftermath provides both encouragement and warning for today's church. For all who are not merely interested but

Foreword

urgently concerned for true revival, this new edition will fill a significant gap in your library, your knowledge and your heart. My prayer, and that of Stanley Griffin, is that the remembrance of a revival that had been almost forgotten will encourage us to pray that God will remember his people and come to us again as he did in 1921.

Brian Edwards, Surbiton, Surrey September 2000

The seeds of this record of revival history were sown in my mind when I was a boy. My mother was showing me a photograph of a silver-haired preacher clutching a Bible to his chest. She told me how the Rev. Douglas Brown had preached in Lowestoft and so many people wanted to hear him that they were sitting on the window-sills of St. John's Church. My father was one of the early converts in the revival, but that knowledge did not make much impression on me at the time.

It was in 1971, when an article appeared in the *Life of Faith* to commemorate the fiftieth anniversary of the East Anglian Revival, that I first wrote about the subject in the *Lowestoft Journal*. Sometime later I began to research the movement in earnest, I discovered that over fifty reports and articles which had appeared in the Christian and secular press had been collected by a former deacon of the Baptist Church who, before he died, had passed them on to the minister. These have been an invaluable source of information.

People who have been personally involved in revival are becoming increasingly rare, but it has been my privilege to know and talk to many who were connected with the movement, chief among these were my parents; but both died before I began to prepare this book. It was exciting to meet MJ Micklewright, deacon emeritus of Westminster Chapel, who, as a young lay- pastor and protege of Douglas Brown visited Lowestoft during the revival and reported on the events for *The Christian*.

The Rev. Robert Browne, Wycliffe Preacher, Baptist Minister and hymn writer, was a local boy of fifteen when he was converted in the revival. My first contact with him came when he was the visiting preacher at the Baptist Church in Lowestoft on the day before I left to do my National Service. He was a great help to me then, and particularly in recent years, he has been a leading eye-witness of the events I have recorded. Finally, I mention the Lowestoft businessman Henry G Hannant, a deacon of the Baptist Church for many years and a member there even before the revival began. Active and alert in his great age, he has been able to give me vivid descriptions of events and personalities.

Although I have a personal interest in the East Anglian revival, my main reason for writing this book is that it was the *last* revival in England! Every revival starts somewhere, and the one which began in Lowestoft in March

1921 soon spread to other parts of East Anglia as it continued throughout the summer. When the Scottish fishermen came to Great Yarmouth for the autumn herring fishing, it broke out with renewed vigour under the preaching of Jock Troup. When they returned to their homes at the end of the season, those fisherfolk carried the revival back to Scotland, only to find that in the meantime God had already begun to move there. It is significant that it was also in the spring of 1921 that the Rev. WP Nicholson began to preach to great crowds in Ulster. This shows how far the revival had spread throughout the United Kingdom at that time, and it is sad to note that, apart from the powerful revival in the Scottish Hebrides in 1949, there has been nothing comparable to it for seventy years. It is of the utmost importance therefore, while it is still within living memory, that this revival should be recorded. Its principles, its strengths and weaknesses, should be considered, so that God's people are stirred to seek Him to revive us again.

Stanley Griffin

Pictured opposite: *Going Fishing* by photographer, Sidney Reynolds

'It is time to seek The Lord'

The first week in March 1921 was the most momentous in the religious life of Lowestoft this century. On Monday afternoon, March 7th, the Rev. A. Douglas Brown arrived by train from London, looking very unwell after spending eleven days in bed with influenza. He was accompanied by the Rev. John Edwards of Brixton because he feared he would not get through the week's meetings. Such an uncertain start to the mission seemed to magnify the grace of God, for not only did Douglas preach with great power on that Monday evening, but literally hundreds more times during the next few months.

Lowestoft, the most easterly town in Britain, flourished in the early years of this century as a sea-port with a prosperous fishing industry. Its popu-

Rev A Douglas Brown

lation was forty four thousand. The old town perched on the cliffs with narrow lanes and steps running steeply down to the north beach. A hundred and twenty feet above the sea stood the upper lighthouse, while the low light, a strong iron structure, was situated on the denes below. South Lowestoft was the newer part of the town with an esplanade running between two piers and fine houses overlooking the sea. A swing bridge across the harbour connected the old and new towns. For the autumn herring fishing, four hundred Scottish herring drifters would join three hundred and fifty local vessels, as well as sailing trawlers and smaller fishing boats. After the First World War the fishing industry decreased because of the worsening economic situation and the over-fishing of the North Sea.

It was now fifty years since the second Evangelical Awakening of 1859. During that time there had been the preaching of Charles Haddon Spurgeon, the campaigns of Dwight L Moody and Ira D Sankey, and the Chapman and Alexander missions. The 1904 revival in Wales had the effect of heightening the desire for, and the expectation of, revival in England. At that time the parish magazines of St. John's Church in Lowestoft carried announcements and reports of special prayer meetings for such a movement of God's Holy Spirit.

On the other hand, during the first two decades of the last century there was religious decline in the nation, in spite of the previous Evangelical Awakening. The authority of the Bible was being undermined by the theory of evolution and what was called 'higher' criticism, which attacked its very origins. Then came the First World War with all its horrors, but even after that there were many people who still believed that man was 'growing up'.

Revival broke out in Lowestoft and other parts of East Anglia under the preaching of the Rev. Douglas Brown of Ramsden Road Baptist Church in

Balham, South London, less than three years after the war. When the movement was at its height in the spring of 1921, the Rev. Henry Martin, Rector of St. Michael's Church in Oulton, Lowestoft, told *The Daily News*: 'The bombardment of Lowestoft five years before and the fear of attack by enemy airships had caused the people to think of religion.' There was an uneasy peace after 1919, during which Lloyd George and his coalition government had trouble abroad, especially when support for the Greeks in their dispute with the Turks brought the threat of another war.

There were even greater problems at home. The boom in employment which immediately followed the end of the war, had given way to gloom and depression, bringing much bitterness. For the ex-servicemen who now found themselves unemployed this was not the 'land fit for heroes to live in' which had been promised. Men in Lowestoft, who had been in the trenches during the war, found that the only work they could obtain was building sea defences. In January 1921 a demonstration for the many unemployed was arranged to take place on the Royal Plain, and to be addressed by the Rector of Lowestoft. It was a flop as only a handful of people turned up. A few months later however, the largest churches in town were crowded with people anxious to hear the Gospel.

Rev Hugh Ferguson

Dr. John Clifford a contemporary of CH Spurgeon, was a notable Baptist leader at the beginning of his ministry and of Douglas Brown at its close. He had earlier embraced a liberal theology, but just before the East Anglian revival he admitted, 'The only hope to rid the churches of the despondency and powerlessness that has taken hold of them is to return to the primitive method of evangelism.' Quoting these words in a sermon, Mr. Brown went on to say, 'I did not expect Dr. Clifford to say anything like that. When I read those words of his, I got down on my knees and re-dedicated my life to God, that wherever

He would send me, whatever He would have me do, I would, God helping me, devote the whole of my life to preaching Jesus Christ and Him crucified, seeking to win men and women to the Saviour.' [1] Clearly, Douglas Brown was encouraged by the Baptist leader's confession.

Spiritual life was clearly evident in Lowestoft before the revival began. In 1917 the Rev. Hugh Ferguson began his ministry in the London Road Baptist Church, where the revival was to begin. Three Anglican churches had evangelical clergymen; the Rev. John Hayes, Vicar of Christ Church; the Rev. William Hardie, Vicar of St. John's, and the Rev. Henry Martin, Rector of St. Michael's in Oulton. The Primitive Methodists in Lowestoft and Oulton were vigorous, though not numerous. John Rushmere, an Oulton Broad coal merchant, town councillor and a lay-preacher, was a Primitive Methodist. There were a number of conversions among the apprentices at the boatyard of JW Brooks. These included Frank Chaplin who was converted in 1920 and later became a missionary in Bolivia, Jack Stringer of Wroxham who stayed in Norfolk, and George Sterry who was baptised as the revival began and became the Sunday School Superintendent and a deacon of the Baptist Church before entering the ministry. There was a good work at the Fishermen's Bethel led by the Port Missionary, Peter Greasley. A young people's Bible Class, which met there every Wednesday evening, was between forty and fifty strong. A London draper, Mr. Boyd, full of evangelistic zeal, had distributed copies of St. John's Gospel during the 1914-1918 war, and had opened the Kirkley Run Mission in the south-west of the town, and the Little Bethel in the Beach Village which lies below the Lowestoft cliffs close to the shore.

Even before the revival a large number of young people were connected with the Baptist Church in London Road and there were strong Bible classes for young men and women. The choir became so large that a platform had to be constructed to extend the rostrum. During this time the church decided to abandon bazaars, sales of work and concerts as means of raising money and to rely only on direct giving. The outstanding feature in the life of the Baptist Church prior to the revival was the weekly prayer meeting. This was held in the school-room on Monday evenings with an attendance of up to ninety people seeking God for a great manifestation of His power, especially among the growing number of young people who were attending the services and Bible classes. The people prayed faithfully in this way for two years. One member, who had prayed most fervently, died just before the revival began. Prayer reached a climax early in 1921.

Hugh Ferguson, who was grieved by the dancing and Sunday concerts that were being sanctioned by the Town Council, was further disturbed by an editorial in *The Lowestoft Journal* on January 15th entitled 'Let Us Pray'. Councillor John Rushmere, supported by Alderman Harris, proposed, 'That the meetings of the Council begin with prayer.' The motion was rejected. The following week the Editor took issue with Mr. Rushmere for bringing the proposal saying, 'Prayer is good, but there are other mental and moral activities that are better.' The editorial prompted Hugh Ferguson to preach a sermon on Job 21:15 entitled, 'What profit is there if we pray?' During the sermon he reminded his congregation: 'All the trouble and confusion in public work today is due to the fact that men are trying to manage in the world without God. Nations and communities who forget God are in a veritable hell of misery, suffering and confusion. The great need of the hour is a truer, deeper and more widespread recognition of God in individual, municipal and national life.' Perhaps even more significant than this sermon was the resolve of Hugh Ferguson and the Rev. John Hayes of Christ Church to pray more urgently that God would work. Just over a month later God answered their prayers.

The title of this chapter comes from Hosea 10:12, 'Break up your fallow ground: for it is time to seek the LORD, till he come and rain righteousness upon you.' This is what the believers did in Lowestoft in 1921, and it is an important principle of revival that while it is always preceded by prayer, it does not originate with prayer but with God. Before the second Evangelical Awakening in 1859 prayer meetings began in Fulton Street New York by Jeremiah Lamphier, in Kells in Ulster by James McQuilkin, and in Wales by Humphrey Jones. Revival is a sovereign work of God, but it is prayed for. In Zechariah 12:10 God promised, 'I will pour upon the house of David, and upon the inhabitants of Jerusalem, the Spirit of grace and of supplication', and the Puritan Matthew Henry comments on that verse: 'When God intends great mercies for His people, the first thing He does is to set them a-praying.'

On Wednesday, July 20th 1921, Hugh Ferguson told the Keswick

Convention about the revival in East Anglia. He described the situation in his church a few months earlier, with its large number of young people and well-attended prayer meetings praying earnestly for revival. 'But I did not know where to find a Missioner,' he confessed. On a rare free Sunday in the autumn of 1920 Ferguson went to Balham to listen to the Rev. Douglas Brown, having heard of the blessing that accompanied his preaching at the Ramsden Road Baptist Church, and he was greatly impressed. Mr. Ferguson had tea with Douglas Brown on Monday afternoon and asked him if he would conduct a series of evangelistic services in Lowestoft, together with a course of Bible readings for Christians. 'Ferguson,' replied Douglas Brown, 'if I can be of any service, I will gladly come. I want no fee but only ask that my expenses be defrayed.' [2] Douglas Brown's subsequent testimony suggests that at the time of Mr. Ferguson's visit he was not as ready to go as his answer implied, and it may have been that very occasion in the autumn of 1920 which was used by God to change the course of Douglas Brown's life and ministry.

Before he arrived in Lowestoft on Monday, March 7th 1921, God had dealt with Douglas Brown in a very powerful way, which he later described at the Keswick Convention in 1922, where he was giving a series of Bible readings on Revival. In one of these addresses entitled, 'A Revitalised Church', he gave an account of God's dealings with him prior to the revival. Douglas began by apologising to the Convention for the fact that he had not had time to prepare his talks. He told them he had addressed seventeen hundred meetings in eighteen months. Certainly this was no exaggeration as his work load was very heavy; in fact, according to *the Christian* he had preached three hundred and seventy times from March to June, and in the *Daily News* it is reported that he had preached three hundred and ten times in eleven weeks.

Preaching from 2 Chronicles 7:14, Douglas Brown illustrated the words, 'If my people shall humble themselves...' from his own experience. He said it had taken four months for that truth to get home to him, even though he had been a minister of the Gospel for twenty six years. It is significant that it was just after Mr. Ferguson's visit that the crisis came. The rest of the story is best told in his own words:

'God laid hold of me in the midst of a Sunday evening service, and He nearly broke my heart while I was preaching. I went back to my vestry and locked the door, and threw myself down on the hearthrug in front of the vestry fireplace broken-hearted. Why? I do not know. My church was filled. I loved my people, and I believe my people loved me. I do not say they ought to, but they did. I was as happy there as I could be. I had never known a Sunday there for fifteen years without conversions. That night I went home and went straight up to my study. My wife came to tell me that supper was ready and was waiting. 'You must not wait supper for me,' I said. 'What is the matter?' she asked. 'I have got a broken heart,' was my reply. It was worth-while having a broken heart for Jesus to mend it. I had no supper that night. Christ laid his hand on a proud minister, and told him that he had not gone far enough, that there were reservations in his surrender, and He wanted him to do a piece of work that he had been trying to evade. I knew what He meant. All November that struggle went on, but I would not give way; I knew God was right, and I knew I was wrong. I knew what it would mean for me, and I was not prepared to pay the price. Then Christmas time came, and all the joy round about seemed to mock me. I knew what Jesus wanted. He showed me pictures of my congregation, and Douglas Brown on his knees in the midst of them. I saw Douglas Brown praying for his own folk, to whom he had preached for over fifteen years. I saw it all in the picture. The struggle went on, and I said to the Lord, 'You know that is not my work. I will pray for anyone else who does it, but please do not give it to me, it will kill me. I cannot get into the pulpit and plead with people. It is against my temperament, and You made me.'

All through January God wrestled with me. There is a love that will not let us go. Glory be to God! At the end of January I was still like poor Jacob, struggling instead of clinging. I thought that what was wrong was my circumstances, when what was really wrong was Douglas Brown. We always put it down to our circumstances as long as we can. It was in February 1921, after four months of struggle that there came the crisis. Oh, how patient God is! On the Saturday night I wrote out my resignation to my church, and it was marked with my own tears. I loved the church, but I felt that if I could not be holy I would be honest; I felt that I could not go on preaching while I had a contention with God. That night the resignation lay on my blotter, and I went to bed but not to sleep. As I went out of my bedroom door in the early hours of the morning I stumbled over my dog. If ever I thanked God for my dog I did that night. As I knelt at my study table, the dog licked his master's face; he thought I was ill; when Mike was doing that I felt that I did not deserve anybody to love me; I felt an outcast.

Then something happened. I found myself in the loving embrace of Christ for ever and ever; and all power and joy and all blessedness rolled in like a deluge. How did it come? I cannot tell you. Perhaps I may when I get to heaven. All explanations are there, but the experience is here. That was two o'clock in the morning. God had waited four months for a man like me; and I said, 'Lord Jesus, I know what you want; You want me to go into mission work. I love Thee more than I dislike that.' I did not hear any rustling of angels' wings. I did not see any sudden light.' 3

Douglas Brown's experience was reminiscent of the American evangelist DL Moody who had to be willing to leave his church in Chicago and preach wherever God led him before the love of God flooded his soul until he had to ask Him to stay His hand.

It was in the same Keswick sermon that Douglas Brown described the other great moulding factor in his life: the influence of his father, who was Minister of the East London Tabernacle when Douglas was a boy. Archibald Brown often took his family to Kessingland, just south of Lowestoft, for their seaside holidays, in the very area where his son was to be so mightily used by God. Douglas Brown related this vivid memory of his father:

'As a little schoolboy of ten, on Friday nights I used to unlace my boots and take them off and creep along from the room where I was supposed to be doing my homework to the door of my father's study. To get to that door I had to go down six steps and every one of them creaked; but even as a little schoolboy I was prepared to spend eight to ten minutes getting down those steps very carefully and cautiously to that door, to listen. Every Friday night father was in his study preparing for Sunday, and he used to pray. What I heard through that keyhole was more wonderful than what I heard from the platform on Sunday morning. I heard a big strong man telling Jesus that he was nothing, that Jesus was everything. I heard the agony of Calvary. I listened to somebody who understood the fellowship of the sufferings of his Lord, until on Friday nights he was, as it were, hanging on the Cross with Jesus: 'I am crucified with Christ: nevertheless I live; yet not I, but Christ liveth in me.' I could not understand it all as a little boy, but it gripped me. I feel the aftermath of it today.'

The testimony of Douglas Brown to his father's influence is concluded by the dedication of a volume of his addresses:

'This volume of addresses I humbly and gratefully dedicate to the memory of my dear father, the Rev. Archibald Brown, whose life and example were a constant and sacred inspiration to me, not only in my early life, but also through the later years, until he fell asleep in Jesus. Whatever blessing has come to other lives through my ministry and revival work I owe, under God, to the inspiration, advice and example of one who, by his fidelity to the truth and loyalty to Christ, awakened in my own heart the Calvary passion for souls, apart from which all preaching fails to reach its highest objective.' 4

These were the events and influences engineered by a sovereign God to prepare His servant for a work of revival in England that has not been repeated. If God prepared a man through childhood into manhood, and then took him away from the scene of a remarkable ministry in London to do greater things in an East Anglian fishing town and beyond, that should be recognised as a work of revival. When Douglas Brown set out for Lowestoft at the beginning of March 1921, he was 'a vessel unto honour, sanctified and meet for the Master's use, and prepared unto every good work.' (2 Tim. 2:21)

The Cloudburst

Hugh Ferguson and his deacons at London Road Baptist Church, were afraid that having arranged a week of meetings they would not get enough people together to make Douglas Brown's visit worthwhile. However, leaflets were distributed throughout the town and the following notice appeared in *The Lowestoft Journal* on Saturday, March 5th: 'The visit is announced of Rev. A. Douglas Brown who will conduct special services in the London Road Baptist Church, Lowestoft from Monday-Friday March 7th-11th inclusive. The evening services are at 7.30 p.m. Mr. Brown, the son of the Rev. Archibald Brown, is a very eminent preacher who has a great message for the times. Full particulars of services are advertised.'

Opened in 1899, the Baptist Church was a splendid preaching auditorium situated in the town centre. It had a fine organ and seated seven hundred and fifty people. The impressive white pulpit supported on three pillars was occupied by a succession of men who were predominantly preachers of the Word of God. On Monday evening the church was well filled. Douglas Brown preached powerfully and there was a spirit of expectancy. On Tuesday a prayer meeting in the morning at eleven, was followed by a Bible reading at three in the afternoon, and another evangelistic service in the evening for which the church was again full. The Holy Spirit's power was felt in the meeting and some said that Douglas Brown had made a great mistake in not appealing for decisions for Christ. Hugh Ferguson described the prayer meeting on Wednesday morning as 'wonderful', and the Bible reading in the afternoon was also very well attended. Here is Ferguson's eye-witness account of the evening meeting when Douglas Brown preached on the healing of the man at the Pool of Bethesda in John chapter 5:

'We had the church packed in the evening. When our brother had delivered his message, he told the people he was going into the vestry and would be glad to see any who wanted help or desired to surrender themselves to Jesus Christ. I shall never forget that night as long as I live. Our brother passed through the deacons' vestry— up a little stairway and into

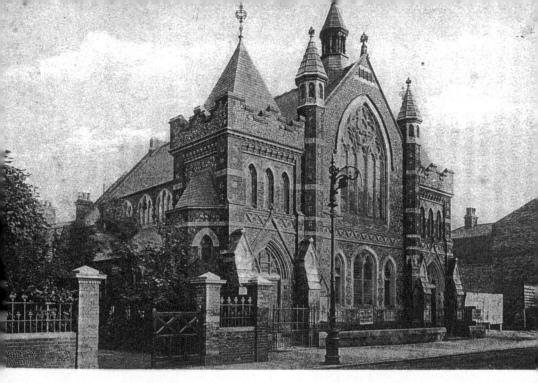

London Road Baptist Church 1921

the pastor's vestry—and he had not been there many minutes when first one came, and then another, and then another. I showed them the way into my little vestry, and then I came down the stairs into the chapel. The people were singing that grand old hymn:

'I hear Thy welcome voice,
 That calls me, Lord, to Thee:
For cleansing in the precious blood
That flowed on Calvary.'

As I entered the church again and stood looking at the people, brother Edwards paused for a moment and asked if there were any others coming into the inquiry-room. We had been praying for 'showers' that night and He gave us a 'cloud-burst'. They came from all parts of the building and filled the deacons' vestry. It was just like waiting outside some theatre; there was one queue down this aisle and another down that. I went to

Douglas Brown and said, "What are we to do? You cannot deal with these people one by one!" So we just opened the schoolroom and in they came— fifty or sixty people to start with. Some of the Christians had the good sense to come with the anxious and help them. I got them together in the schoolroom and began to speak to them in a company. I had been speaking for only a few minutes, the door opened and another batch came in, and all was confusion for a few minutes. Then I tried to speak to them again; and again the door opened and another batch came in. It was a wonderful sight. We got those who had definitely surrendered to Christ to keep on one side; and those who had difficulties we put into classrooms with a good Christian worker to help them and deal with them. Presently there was quietness, and that night between sixty and seventy of my dear young people, those we had been praying to God for—young men and women, from the ages of fifteen to twenty—some sixty or seventy of them that night 'passed from death to life'.' [1]

One convert that night was Robert Browne, a young lad of fifteen years, who gave his version of the events of that memorable night:

'I had connections with the Baptist Church and used to walk from my home in Oulton Broad with my pal to the Bible Class. It was so large that two rooms were hired in the old technical college, one for the young men's class and one for the young ladies' class. I was one of a large company of young men from fourteen years of age upwards. On the first Sunday in March the leader of our class, the late Mr. E G Baley, asked 'his boys' as he called us, to do something for him that week. 'I want you to come to these special services, come down one night, come down on Tuesday.' Someone said, 'Yes, we'll come.' And so I remember that on the Tuesday night I went with my friend and took part in this gospel service. There were hymns and prayers and Douglas Brown spoke; nothing particular happened but there was the sense of the moving of God's Spirit. I remember how the next day my pal came along as I was digging my father's allotment. 'Hey! You going down to the meeting again tonight?' he asked. 'I think I shall go.' 'I'll come with you,' I replied. The Wednesday night was an occasion that many will never forget. At the conclusion of his address, Mr. Brown appealed for those who wished to know more about Christian things to come forward. The aisles were immediately filled with people, I was among them, so was my friend, and many other young people connected with the church. As I remember, we went down the aisle, up by the organ and up a staircase into the schoolroom, which was packed with inquirers; they were not all young people but older people as well. That was the night when I first knew what it was to have true faith in Christ. I knew very little, just as every new convert knows very little, but I knew sufficient of the facts and I had trusted Christ as my Saviour.'

On the Thursday evening the meeting was transferred to the Fishermen's Bethel, not more than a hundred yards from the Baptist Church towards the Fishmarket. It was the annual meeting of the Bethel; Hugh Ferguson was in the chair and greetings and reports were on the programme and Douglas Brown would preach. The building was packed and the atmosphere was charged with Spiritual power as the people waited for blessing. 'This is not an atmosphere for figures,' remarked the Treasurer as he gave his report in about three minutes! Douglas Brown was soon in the pulpit, and having been in the service of the *White Star Shipping Line*, he was quite at home in the nautical surroundings. He preached on the words of Peter, 'If it be Thou, bid me come to Thee on the water.' He showed that stepping down from the boat and stepping on the water was like casting off all human dependence, stepping on the Word of God and coming to Christ. Hugh Ferguson takes up the story again:

'The inquiry room was packed a few minutes after the sermon, with men and women crying to God, 'What must we do to be saved?' It was like an auction room. There was my brother the Rev. John Hayes, Vicar of Christ Church, dealing with anxious souls, and the Rev. John Edwards of Brixton standing on another form, and I was standing with some others, and we were all engaged in the glorious work of pointing men and women to Christ. The place was so packed that when you got in you could not alter your position. The missioner had simply to tell the people, "You will have to come to Christ where you are." That night they were coming to Jesus all over the building.' [2]

After another great meeting in the Baptist Church on Friday it was obvious that God was moving in a remarkable way and more room would need to be made for the blessing to continue. Douglas Brown had to return to his church in Balham for the Sunday services, but before he left, Hugh Ferguson, John Hayes and Peter Greasley, Port Missionary and leader of the Bethel, met together and decided to tear up their programmes and do as the Spirit of God led. It was arranged therefore, that Douglas Brown would return to Lowestoft the following Monday.

On March 17th the first of three reports appeared in *The Christian* entitled 'Revival Times in Lowestoft' by MJ Micklewright. Formerly a member of the church in Balham where Douglas Brown was pastor, he was now a lay pastor himself in East London. Having been unwell and hearing of the blessing that had broken out at Lowestoft, he obtained leave from his employment and went to see what great things God was doing. When, early in the second week, Douglas Brown saw Micklewright in one of the meetings he said, 'The Lord sent you here, I want you for my 'curate'.' Montague Micklewright's task was to collect names and requests and list them for the prayer meetings, which were held in the Baptist Church each morning. After a short address by Mr. Brown, requests for prayer were read out. So numerous were these requests that they had to be divided into three sections, one for the morning prayer session, another for the afternoon Bible reading, and the third group for the evening meeting. Prayers were made daily for the salvation of souls; husbands, wives, children, parents, friends and neighbours were brought before the Throne of Grace. 'It was great to hear the sobs through those prayers, as they cried to God for the salvation of those who were lost,' commented Ferguson. One old man would stand out in the aisle of the church during those prayer meetings, lift his hand to heaven and cry, 'O Lord, save!'

As the people prayed in Lowestoft they knew that in other places, such as the Ramsden Road Church, Balham, and the Metropolitan Tabernacle, people were praying for a mighty out-pouring of the Holy Spirit on Lowestoft and beyond. When Douglas Brown returned to Balham for the weekend of March 19th-21st, he told the Saturday evening prayer meeting of the work of God in Lowestoft. The same spirit of prayer that he had experienced in the East Anglian fishing port descended on that meeting also. 'We took it as an earnest of coming blessing,' wrote Montague Micklewright. 'The following Sunday and Monday witnessed an open confession of faith on the part of scores of persons—some of them adults of mature age, the remainder children and young people. During the week in Lowestoft, upon a moderate statement, about eighty persons entered the

Dockers at work, Lowestoft 1921

inquiry rooms at the Baptist Church from Tuesday to Friday, and among them some very striking cases of conversion.'

After that first memorable week it was decided to widen the influence of the meetings, and so from the second week the afternoon Bible readings were held at Christ Church. The first one filled the Parish Room, the next one filled the church, and so it continued for three weeks, including Easter week, as Douglas Brown gave Bible studies on the personal return of the Lord Jesus Christ. On those memorable afternoons the tramcars were full of people carrying Bibles, and when they reached Old Nelson Street the conductor would call out, 'Get off here for Christ Church.' Someone said that the addresses were like 'bombshells'; their aim was practical and they were directed at the lives of Christians. 'Two stand out in the memory of all,' reported Micklewright. 'They were on "The Judgement Seat of

Christ". Solemn words were spoken in regard to some classes of worker—including the preacher— who had occupied his time with a social gospel or philosophical discourse, and the Sunday School teacher or Bible Class leader who had been an unfaithful steward of the Word. Those services maintained the same wonderful attendances and earnestness, and on Good Friday afternoon, notwithstanding the brilliant sunshine and services in most other churches, Christ Church was more crowded than ever.'

The outstanding feature of this spiritual movement was the preaching of the Gospel. Unlike the more famous Welsh revival seventeen years earlier, when at times and in some places the preaching was drowned by the singing and other phenomena, in East Anglia the preaching was predominant. Although the evening meetings were formal, with Douglas Brown preaching in an academic gown, he preached simply on the basic truths of the Christian faith from Scripture, with the Cross central to every message. 'Douglas Brown preaches the truth with no uncertain sound,' said Hugh Ferguson. 'Ruin by the Fall, Redemption by the Atoning Blood, Regeneration and Renewal by the Holy Ghost, Anointing by the Holy Ghost for Service, Godly Living, Waiting for the Return of the Lord Jesus Christ from Heaven. You get old Bible doctrines and Apostolic preaching and, thank God, Apostolic results.' [3] There does not appear to have been the musical support that is so important to modern evangelistic campaigns, although the hymn singing from Sankey's *Sacred Songs* was immensely popular. People came in their hundreds night after night to hear the preacher and his message. 'He was different from anybody else I ever heard,' said one octogenarian looking back on those days. 'It was as though he was speaking to me personally.' Standing outside Boots the chemists, where the Baptist Church had stood in 1921, the old man recalled, 'Oh the singing! You could hear it out here; it drew the people in.'

'My father took me to the meetings; I was twelve at the time,' a lady recounted, 'but I can hear Douglas Brown now: "The woman left her water pot, and went her way into the city, and said to the men, Come see a Man which told me all things that ever I did: is not this the Christ?" (John 4:28-29) 'I also heard him preach on Jesus going up to the cross,' she continued. 'He kept pointing, you could see it all, it was so touching.' Another lady who was converted at that time remembered Douglas Brown preaching on the cross. 'His hair was white, his face was radiant, I felt he was speaking to me alone.'

An elderly widow, who was a girl in the Wesleyan Bible Class at the time of the revival, went to the meetings in the Baptist Church. 'I remember Douglas Brown preaching on the Cross and describing the nails with tears,' she said. 'I think the organist left the organ and went to the inquiry room. My Bible class leader touched me on the shoulder and spoke to me. I wept, and then I went out. It was for re-dedication because I was already converted.'

'I want you to come to the Baptist Church to hear a preacher tonight,' a mother said to her son one day in March 1921. Sixty years later he described the scene. 'The church was full and Douglas Brown preached on "The Left Water Pot". As he neared the end of his address, and while he was still preaching, one or two people left their seats and went to the communion rail, and by the time the service was over people were standing all round it.'

Many exciting stories of conversions were recorded during those weeks, some involving whole families. A mother who was converted during the first week immediately put in a request for prayer for her son, who was preparing to emigrate to Canada. A few days later one of her daughters was converted and this was followed the next evening by the son who had been prayed for. He was well-known in the district, and at Douglas Brown's request he testified to his new-found faith the following evening and concluded by inviting other young men present to give their hearts to God. A companion of his who was in the congregation was quite overwhelmed by this testimony and tried to get away from the building. He was followed by one of the workers, who spoke to him about his soul. Before the evening was over he was on his knees with Mr. Brown in the vestry committing his life to Christ. Thus, the conversion of three members of a family and a friend in quick succession was seen as the immediate and dramatic answer to prayer.

The Rev. John Hayes described the scenes in Christ Church in March 1921.

'I want to take you into my church one Wednesday evening. At a quarter to seven that church is full, it is 'bung' full, and I have to go up in the pulpit and say to the people, "My friends, I want those of you who love the Lord Jesus to go out. I want you to go into the Parish Hall and pray." They got up and went, here and there all over the church; they passed into the Parish Hall, some two hundred of them gathered there, and they held a prayer meeting. Then I had to say to the young men, "I want you to get up and sit on the floor at the front": and we had to get people into that church packed in that way, and in the vestry. In the Parish Hall they were praying; there was a sister praying for her sister who was in the church, and at the close of the service that sister came to me and said, 'I want to talk to you." On the following Tuesday evening that sister was led to Christ in my study in answer to the prayer offered in the Parish Hall.

We can never tell you half of the answers to prayer. It has been most wonderful. Young men praying for the girls to whom they were engaged, girls praying for their young men, mothers praying for their boys and their girls, children praying for their fathers, friends praying for friends. I remember one night in the church there stood a young man with bowed head, and I said, 'What are you doing here?' 'I have been praying for my five companions, and four of them have come to Jesus, and I am praying for the last one; he has not come tonight. I do not know whether he came. I have not heard the end of the story, but that is what has been going on." 4

A woman whose life and marriage were broken, crept into the back of one of the churches where the meetings were being held and listened to the gospel. She came back night after night but she was afraid to respond because of the state of her life. At last she came and brought her husband with her; they came to Christ together and their marriage was restored. John Hayes had shaken hands with that woman as she walked down the aisle and said, 'I am so glad to see you here tonight.' He did not know who she was until she came into the vestry and said, 'I want Jesus Christ.' At the London Road Baptist Church one evening, a man who had come into the inquiry room and found peace with God was worried at the thought of telling his wife. Meanwhile, in another room a woman was being counselled. Both wondered how they would tell their respective partners about this, the greatest experience of their lives. They needn't have worried, they were husband and wife and they met on the premises before they went home, after coming to the meeting separately!

A man was kneeling on the pavement outside the Fishermen's Bethel one evening. Douglas Brown saw him and, thinking he was in trouble of soul, approached him to speak with him. 'O sir,' he said, 'don't disturb me: I've been praying for my boys for years, and the three of them are in the inquiry room, thank God!' Two professional men who were related and well-known in the town were converted on successive evenings. Two women of low repute knelt at the communion rail one night and were heard to cry, 'O God! O God!' On another evening a powerful man who had a criminal record, and against whom the leaders had been warned, came into the church. He came into the vestry with the words, 'I want God,' and knelt at the communion rail with a little girl of thirteen years as each received the Saviour. The man immediately joined himself with a band of open-air preachers and went all over the town confessing Christ as his Saviour. He soon brought two of his friends to the meetings who were also led to the Lord.

Douglas Brown and Hugh Ferguson were crossing the harbour bridge late one evening after a meeting when they came across a man who, attempting to speak to them, broke down, leaned over the railings and wept like a child. He was under deep conviction of sin and felt he was too bad to be saved. The two ministers took him aside and there on the pavement beside the bridge led him to Christ. The next evening he was first down the aisle as a testimony to his new found faith. On Good Friday morning a man was loitering on the sea front outside the hotel dining-room where Douglas Brown was having breakfast. The Holy Spirit prompted him to go and speak to the man, so he went out and joined him on one of the seats. He remarked on the 'lovely' morning and 'glorious' sea. 'Yes, and what a glorious Saviour you have,' was the quick reply. He was an anxious soul and he was pointed to Christ there on that seat on the sea front.

A poor desperate woman, whose family had recently died, was passing the Baptist Church one evening; bare-footed and hatless she was about to throw herself into the harbour. Arrested by the sound of singing she slipped into the back of the church. Although she found no rest or peace that evening and went away stating her intention of not returning, the Spirit drew her, and the following evening she was again in the congregation and came to Christ. Snatched from the verge of suicide she became the caretaker of the Baptist Church for many years.

A builder, whose drunken ways created havoc in his home and almost drove his poor afflicted wife to suicide, was converted, together with his wife. Afterwards, instead of going to the public house, the man would push his wife to the services and prayer meetings in her invalid chair, where they would thank God for His mercy and pray for their children who had been affected by the evil influences formerly in their home. John Hayes commented, 'There have been times when Mr. Ferguson and I have gone alone and sobbed out our hearts together in joy at the great things God has done for us.'

People from the seaside village of Kessingland four miles south of Lowestoft would bus, cycle or walk into the town for the meetings. A number of appeals were sent to Douglas Brown to preach in the village but it was impossible to arrange a visit during the first two weeks, so a message was sent to the people to devote themselves to prayer. A visit to Kessingland Bethel was arranged for the Thursday evening of the third week. The preacher delivered his message and had only ten minutes to spare before returning to Lowestoft to preach. Nevertheless, there were a number of professions of conversion and there are people in Kessingland today who remember that time.

On Saturday, 26th March 1921 a pressman who worked for a London newspaper was home on holiday and walking down a Suffolk lane when he heard a voice telling him to take a turning to the right. He had not gone far when he met a man carrying a carpet bag, walking miserably with his head bowed. The man looked up and recognised the printer saying, 'I saw you at one of the meetings!' 'Yes, I have been to some of the meetings,' the man replied. The man with the bag told his story: 'Eleven years ago I left in disgrace. I have been in South Africa for eight years and I have only been back in England a few weeks. I have never been near a house of God and I felt I would just fling myself out of life. But last Wednesday my wife said to me, 'I am going to one of the services and I want you to come too.' When she said that, I took up a book and flung it at her head. 'Well,' she said, 'You can do what you will, but a voice has told me to go and I'm going.'' That woman went to the meeting, and so did her reluctant and ill-tempered husband. On Saturday the man was wandering down that country lane under conviction of sin. He was soon kneeling in the lane with his new friend, and the burden of his sin was lifted. They went home and later that day the man's wife was converted. The following day the pressman wrote to Douglas Brown and told him that at quarter to nine that evening there would be a little prayer meeting in a wood where a husband and wife, with three friends who had been converted the day before, and himself would give thanks "for God's good work, the miracle of grace'.

During the last week of March, the meetings which had previously been held in the Baptist Church, Christ Church and the Bethel, moved to St. John's Church where the vicar, the Rev. William Hardie, supported the work of revival. St. John's, which was situated just south of the harbour bridge, seated eleven hundred people and its spire was a landmark in the centre of the town. Sadly, only Christ Church and the Bethel still remain today. The London Road Baptist Church moved to Kirkley and its former magnificent preaching auditorium was demolished in 1974 to make way for Boots and a pedestrian precinct. The parish of St. John's was amalgamated with St. Peter's at Kirkley when the church building, which was filled to overflowing in those revival days, was also demolished. The fourth week of the revival saw the best attended meetings of all, with the numbers increased by people coming in from the surrounding neighbourhood. The evening services were preceded by open-air meetings at six o'clock. Even today, more than seventy years later, there are those who say of those services in the church, 'Oh it was wonderful! There were people everywhere, on the window sills, round the font, on the pulpit steps and in the aisles.' Others claim, 'I 'came out' at St. John's.'

'On the Thursday night of the fourth week it was a wonderful sight,' said Hugh Ferguson. 'An hour before the service was due to begin the great building was packed, and at the close we thanked God for many who had passed from death into life and realised Christ as their own personal Saviour.' One man, who was young at the time, told the writer how he saw one and another kneeling by the hedgerows as he walked home to Oulton Broad from St. John's. The final meeting on the Friday evening was to have been held at the Baptist Church where it all began, but Mr. Ferguson knew it would be impossible to accommodate all the people there, so he and Mr. Hardie decided it should be held at St. John's.

As on the previous evening, every conceivable space in the church was taken long before the service was due to begin, and there were still people outside. In many respects that final service was a summary of all that had happened throughout that memorable month. The four ministers in the pulpit were wonderfully united in the Gospel: the Baptists, Douglas Brown and Hugh Ferguson, and the Anglicans, John Hayes and William Hardie. The congregation included people from every kind of church, and from no church at all. Among them were Anglicans, Nonconformists, Salvation Army, Brethren and those who attended the Railway Mission. 5 There were even Christian Scientists who, as Mr. Ferguson said, 'Got converted and when they got Christ they broke from Christian Science.' Singing had featured in all the meetings throughout the month. Some of the gospel hymns from Sankey's collection had been sung time and time again: 'I am coming Lord', 'Come to the Saviour now', and 'Blessed be the fountain of blood', which came to be known as the hymn of the revival. On that last evening St. John's Church and its vicinity echoed with the strains of 'What a Friend we have in Jesus'. The organist was thrilled to play for such a meeting and his choir that evening, singing from the chancel, included many fishermen. They sang the version with the chorus:

'I love Jesus, hallelujah,
I love Jesus, yes I do.'

They held onto that chorus two or three times. Another unforgettable moment was the singing by that great congregation of 'God be with you till we meet again', joined by the crowds in the street outside. It was the same simple, direct gospel message which was again preached on that last evening; the gospel of man's ruin through sin, and his salvation through Christ and His blood shed on Calvary.

There were remarkable scenes on Saturday morning, April 2nd as Mr. Brown left Lowestoft. A number of groups had assembled in the station booking hall and he went to each, bidding them farewell and committing them to God in prayer. A crowd of workers and converts gathered on the platform, together with Hugh Ferguson, John Hayes and William Hardie, and just as the train left Mr. Hardie struck up a verse of 'God be with you till we meet again'. When the train reached Oulton Broad South another crowd, including many converts, was waiting on the station. Douglas

Brown shook hands with as many as possible and committed them to God in prayer before the train bore him homewards to London. And so, what began as a five day mission among young people at the Baptist Church, a month later was concluded in this way.

On Monday, April 4th, a church business meeting was held at London Road Baptist Church, at which the resolution to send this message to the Baptist Church at Ramsden Road, Balham, was moved by Mr. A B Cooper:

'We desire to record our sense of the great debt of gratitude we owe you, the officers and members of the Baptist Church at Ramsden Road, Balham, for your generosity and self-sacrifice in giving up to us and God's cause in Lowestoft the services of your beloved Pastor, the Rev. Douglas Brown.

We should not have dared to accept so great a sacrifice on your part, had we not such convincing evidence that God was mightily using him for the ingathering of souls. We thank God for all that this past month has meant to ourselves and to so many others. It has been a time of real revival and we trust and believe the beginning of a still greater harvest. By his clear and fearless proclamation of God's word, by the tireless devotion which led him to spend and be spent, and by his winsome personality and Christ-like spirit, he has won an abiding place in our love and esteem.

We pray that God may continually bless and use him in his ministry at his own church, and that you, together with him, may receive again in spiritual blessing a hundredfold for that which you have given. We thank you for your prayers during the past months, and feel that the work which we have mutually shared during this great mission has created a strong and loving tie between ourselves and you.

You will rejoice to know that we have a record of more than five hundred converts, who have come from many churches during the mission and there must be many more of whom we have not heard particulars.'

Writing in *The Churchman's Magazine*, the Rev. Henry Martin reported, 'A very memorable converts' gathering was held some three weeks after the close of the first section of meetings.' This would have been in mid-April. The Baptist Church was filled for the occasion and three-quarters of the congregation consisted of young people who had responded to the invitation cards which had been sent out. 'For an hour the prayer and praise of these young Christians filled hearts with joy and eyes with tears.'

The showers continue

Although Douglas Brown had returned to London after preaching at least twice each day from Monday to Friday throughout March, his ministry in Lowestoft was not yet finished. He returned during Whitsun week before preaching at missions in Ipswich, Yarmouth, Norwich and Cambridge, and again for one day at the end of July, and then for a week of convention meetings in September.

There was a remarkable movement of the Spirit of God in the Lowestoft area during Whitsun week. Due to address a meeting at St. Michael's Church, Oulton on Tuesday afternoon, Douglas Brown arrived unexpectedly on Monday because of the uncertainty of the train service. He strolled along the sea front but he was soon recognised and persuaded to preach at the Salvation Army open-air meeting. A large crowd gathered and Mr. Brown had the double joy of preaching the gospel and seeing a number of souls come to faith in Christ. That evening he attended the prayer meeting at the Baptist Church, which was held on Monday even when it was a Bank Holiday. Douglas Brown spoke helpfully to Christian workers and then, at about nine o'clock, they went round to the Salvation Army Citadel where he preached again and souls were saved.

Douglas subsequently told of a girl who had been converted on the sands that afternoon and who had gone home and testified to her new found faith. Her parents had laughed at her, but her sister had said, 'If there is a service anywhere tonight, I'll go with you.' 'Yes there is,' the convert replied, 'but it is at the Salvation Army Citadel.' 'I don't care where it is, I'll go,' said the sister. She went to the meeting at the Citadel and was converted. 'That is the kind of movement we want,' declared Douglas Brown. 'We don't want excitement, we don't want noise, we want the simple methods of Jesus Christ; and we have often proved, brothers and sisters, that where we have laid the foundation of believing prayer, and have taken God's Holy Word and preached it in dependence upon the Holy Spirit, there has been nothing but victory all along the line and it is not finished yet.'

On Tuesday afternoon Douglas Brown addressed a large congregation

Lowestoft Sea Front in the 1920s

at Oulton Parish Church. The plan for this week was for Douglas Brown to preach in the villages around Lowestoft in the evenings from Tuesday to Friday, and on the Tuesday evening a meeting was held at Holly Farm, Blundeston. A large barn was filled to overflowing as the gospel was preached in this small village which lies just to the north-west of Lowestoft.

A report in *The Christian* claimed that the services in Lowestoft during Whitsun week were the most remarkable of the whole series; this was certainly true of the Thursday afternoon service in Oulton Parish Church. Standing on the edge of the marshes, the Norman church of St. Michael with its central tower and a chancel as long as the nave, was full. Mr. Brown gave a heart-searching address on the three anointings of King David. At the close he said that it had been laid on his heart and on the heart of the Rector, to re-dedicate themselves to God, 'in thankfulness for all the great spiritual uplift and soul-humbling experiences of the past months'. As the last hymn 'When I Survey the Wondrous Cross' was being sung, Mr. Brown and Mr. Ferguson, with the Rector of Oulton and the

Vicars of Christ Church and St. John's Lowestoft, and the Congregational Minister, the Rev. J Butterworth, went to the communion table and knelt. Silently and spontaneously three-quarters of the congregation followed, kneeling at the front, down the chancel, past the tower and down the nave. This is how Henry Martin, the Rector, described the close of the meeting to *The Christian*:

'As the last verse of the hymn, 'Were the whole realm of nature mine', was being sung, the hush of the Holy Ghost fell on the hearts of all: it was an experience to be entered into but not described. The hymn ended and in words of consecrating prayer and praise the offering of these hundreds of lives was presented for Divine acceptance. The crowd of joyful, tear-marked faces was an attestation to the quiet joy and peace that followed on this act of devotion. A memorable service thus came to its close, to be followed by lingering groups in the old churchyard whose one subject of conversation was this new found joy.' [1]

Henry Martin reported in another journal:

'Ministers in the vestry with hearts too full for words could only wring each other's hands as they wept together tears of joy.' [2]

There was a remarkable prelude to that afternoon in Oulton Parish Church. Douglas Brown was staying at the Rectory during this week of meetings, and in the early hours of Thursday morning he was awakened by a voice saying, 'Thou shalt see greater things than these.' (John 14:12) He slipped quietly down to the study to pray and soon the door opened and the Rector appeared. He too had been awakened and had received the same message from John's Gospel. It had also been on Mr. Brown's mind to make a public act of praise, thanksgiving and self-consecration at the afternoon service.

On Thursday evening something similar happened at the Union Chapel in Somerleyton, a delightful old-world English village a few miles from Lowestoft. Shortly before the service an open-air meeting was held on the picturesque village green. In the chapel Douglas Brown invited short prayers from the believers who had gathered, and then delivered an informal address. After preaching he said that he and Mr. Ferguson would kneel in an

Scottish fisherman at Lowestoft

act of re-dedication and invited other Christians to join them. He then invited those who wished to respond to Christ to come also. Middle-aged and elderly responded, while country lads and girls came forward and knelt with them. It was reported that a publican and his wife were converted, went back home and tipped their barrels of beer on the marshes!

The last meeting of this village week was held in Oulton Church Institute, which an hour before time was crowded to the doors, as also was a small Primitive Methodist Chapel adjoining, and an open-air audience of very considerable size. To each of these gatherings Mr. Brown spoke, and souls were led to Christ.

Lowestoft Swing Bridge 1897-1969

After the moving service at St. Michael's Church on Thursday it is not surprising that the Holy Spirit was still at work there on Sunday. At the end of the morning service Henry Martin, the Rector, closed his Bible and appealed for conversions. Soon the Rector's wife was busy in the vestry leading ladies of the parish to Christ. In the afternoon the Rector walked across to the church and found a crowd of people there 'who wanted to get near Jesus'. It was impossible to hold the normal Sunday School so the afternoon was spent in the church with young and old joining in praise and prayer. What a Sunday that was, with spiritual blessing affecting the whole district! That evening the Primitive Methodists in Oulton closed their chapel and went as a body to the Parish Church where there was another soul-stirring service. Douglas Brown's preaching had made a considerable impact on the Primitive Methodist congregation at Oulton with a number of conversions, including almost the whole of the young people's Bible class.

Frank Chaplin, who had been an apprentice at the boat yard when he was converted as a young man, was a missionary in Guatemala in 1971 when he read a letter in *The Lowestoft Journal* commemorating the fiftieth anniversary of the revival. He replied to that letter, giving some of his first-hand impressions:

'Let me tell you something of myself and those momentous days of 1921. I was converted to Christ in November 1920. I had completed my twentieth year. In February of 1921 I lost my job as a boat-builder because of the slack conditions in the trade. I had gone to Wroxham to work, when the revival broke out in Lowestoft. However at Easter that year I came home for a few days. I found out that the meetings were still going on. I went to the Good Friday afternoon at Christ Church and heard the Rev. A. Douglas Brown for the first time. I well remember the message that day. I had never heard anything like it before. He spoke from Ephesians 5:25-27 on Christ and the true church. I went to every meeting during that weekend and was greatly blessed.'

When my work terminated in Wroxham I returned home to Oulton Broad, and although out of work most of that year I entered into the spirit of the revival. All of that summer the interest continued. I well remember the meeting in Oulton Parish Church on the Thursday afternoon of Whitsun week that you referred to. The Rector of those days, Rev. Henry Martin, was a great man of God, and when I left my homeland for missionary work in the country of Bolivia, he gave me a fine farewell meeting in the parish hall. I was not a member of his church but had been baptised in August 1921 and taken into fellowship at London Road Baptist Church by Pastor Hugh P Ferguson. My memory of those momentous days is quite fresh and one would long to see such a movement of the Spirit of God in our day and generation.'

The Press
As the period of Douglas Brown's intensive preaching in Lowestoft drew to a close and he moved to other towns in East Anglia, reports about the revival appeared in *Daily News*. The first one opened with a paragraph from a letter written by the Rev. Henry Martin of St. Michael's Oulton to Balham Baptist Church.

'I want to say that no-one who has not had the hallowed joy of sharing in this movement, which is in no sense localised to one town, can have any idea of the miracles of grace that are being wrought. I wish many of you could have been with us this week. It has seen village work in—barns, churches, chapels and institutes crowded beyond their capacity, and souls saved by the score. Without fee or reward Mr. Douglas Brown—who is the son of the well-known Baptist preacher, Rev. Archibald Brown—has during the past eleven weeks addressed 310 meetings, and the conversions are stated to number over a thousand. Petitions for prayer have numbered nearly 300 on a single day.'

'What do you think of the revival in East Anglia?' a reporter asked the Rev. Henry Martin. 'It is the biggest thing I have ever seen,' he replied. 'People have come from the whole of the surrounding area to attend the meetings. We did not advertise extensively, nor was there any organisation. It was just as if the Spirit of God had made plans and carried them through. Gatherings held by the Rev. A. Douglas Brown were entirely free from excitement. He is not hysterical but a preacher who gives a clear presentation of the Gospel. The conversions are genuine, and some of those in Lowestoft were especially striking.' The report concluded with a paragraph headed 'The New Lowestoft': 'I think,' said Henry Martin, 'That probably the experience of the bombardment of Lowestoft by the Germans five years ago, and almost daily fear of attack by enemy airships, caused the people to think of religion in a way they never did before.'

Councillor John Rushmere, a leading Primitive Methodist made the following comment: 'Friends have told me that not long since, they feared that ugly things might happen in the town because of the temper of some of the people. All is now quite different they say, and the revival is the cause.'

Another report in *Daily News* described the generosity of Christians as a fruit of the revival. The Rev. WG Hardie, Vicar of St. John's Lowestoft, told the reporter that during the previous two months the ordinary offerings at his church had increased by fifty per cent. 'They had a debt of £600. Without previous warning he announced a meeting to receive the accounts and answer questions. He also stated that he would sit in his vestry to receive gifts a day or two later. About a hundred people were present at the meeting, and quite spontaneously £300 was promised. On the gift day, from 10 am until 8 pm., so continuous was the stream of givers—professional people, shop assistants, domestic servants, Sunday school children—that he could not go home to a meal. He secured the whole of the £600, and since then another £120 had come in.' The report continued, 'The Rev. John Hayes, Vicar of Christ Church, assured me that there was no emotional appeal, cheap sensationalism, or manufactured revivalism. He thought Mr. Brown's addresses were just such as he might have preached to his own congregation.' He explained how the clergy had not intended to take a prominent part in the meetings when they started in the Baptist Church. Out of courtesy he offered the accommodation of his parish hall, and when that overflowed he opened his church.

The final report in *Daily News* described what it called the 'Close of the Campaign', when meetings were held in the Baptist Church in the afternoon and evening on a Friday in July.

'The building was crowded to its capacity long before the services commenced. Addresses of appreciation were given by several friends including the Salvation Army Adjutant and the Rev. Henry Martin, who conducted the service and said that they were expecting greater things in the future, although they had already seen marvellous things. Mr. Brown thanked all those who had supported his efforts and expressed his pleasure that the services had drawn together the Christians in the town and had achieved his chief object of bringing men and women to Christ. He then went on to say that there must be a revival in the land or there would be revolution. If there was not a revival in the churches, they would not count in ten years time.

In our history, ethical revival had always been preceded by evangelical revival, and people all over the land were praying for the latter. He wanted to see men and women made comfortable but it was not his job to preach that from the pulpit; he was called to preach the gospel of Christ. Mr. Brown then asked those in the church who had received definite benefit during the past five months to stand up, and the bulk of those present stood, to be directly addressed by him. He next appealed to those in the congregation who might not have made the great decision and reminded them that it was his five hundred and third appeal. During the meeting hope was expressed that there would be a week's convention in September in which Mr. Brown would take part.'

An East Anglian Revival

On Friday, May 27th, Montague Micklewright, who had helped Douglas Brown at Lowestoft, was ordained to the Christian ministry at Major Road Baptist Church, Stratford. Douglas Brown, his pastor at Balham, preached at that ordination service and the report of his address reveals the thrust of his ministry:

'Clearly the times in which we live have gripped him, but more than that, the unchangeable gospel of Christ holds him fast. Hence he is out of patience with a dead moderatism, also with doctrinal compromise. Is it to be revolution or regeneration? The question haunts many minds today, and many are content to wait and see. Mr. Brown however, calls men to Calvary, to repentance unto life, to the new birth. And to believers he has a word of abounding freshness from inspired prophecy. With him, the blessed hope of the Lord's return is not a negligible theory of things. 'Whosoever hath this hope in him, purifieth himself.' (1 John 3:3) As a nation we have turned our back upon God. As organised churches, we have put our programmes in place of the Holy Spirit. We must get back to the primal message of the cross, to the simple evangelistic message of the Master himself, and to the prayer of faith. Some seem to be afraid of emotion. As a matter of fact the church is dying for want of emotion! In eloquent terms the preacher called his hearers back to Calvary and its implications in a regenerated life, and his appeal was made urgent in the solemn declaration that 'the coming of the Lord draweth nigh!' [1]

The regular prayer meeting was held at Ramsden Road on Saturday, May 28th, and Douglas Brown was in his own pulpit in Balham on the Sunday. It was on that same day that there was the remarkable display of fervour and unity amongst Christians at Oulton, near Lowestoft, described in the previous chapter. Meetings began in Ipswich on the Monday. It is one of the features of true revival that God moves in different places at the same time.

Ipswich, Monday May 30th - Friday June 3rd
The meetings continued on the same lines as those held at Lowestoft in March. A prayer meeting in the morning was followed by a Bible reading in

the afternoon and an evangelistic service in the evening. The venue was Burlington Baptist Church whose pastor, the Rev. Louis Parkinson, was eager to have meetings in Ipswich. He had the enthusiastic support of Canon Herbert Hinde, Vicar of St. John's and a convinced evangelical, and also of the Rev. John Patten, Minister of Tacket Street Congregational Church. No particular preparations had been made and the meetings were not extensively advertised, although there had been preparations of a deeper kind. For more than a year, free church ministers had met weekly to pray for revival. There had been prayer meetings for many years on Friday afternoons for the same object, and cottage meetings in connection with the church had been going on for many months. Louis Parkinson had been to Lowestoft to give Bible addresses, and Hugh Ferguson had been to Ipswich to give an account of the revival in Lowestoft. A series of Advent Testimony meetings in Ipswich, at which Douglas Brown should have been the speaker, was cancelled, leaving the way open for the historic meetings that were about to begin.

The *Daily News* carried a report of the first meeting headed: 'Brake Loads Coming'. It described the meeting as quiet and undemonstrative, 'with hymns of a devotional rather than a revivalist type'. Before the meeting began a telegram from Lowestoft was read: 'Lowestoft sends heartiest greetings and best wishes for a great ingathering.' According to *The Christian* the first meeting was unforgettable. 'Eleven hundred people filled the church; Mr. Brown's sermon was on revival and what it means; and at the close two hundred and fifty Christians rose in reponse to an appeal to give themselves to God in a new dedication.'

It was soon evident that this was another movement of the Holy Spirit. The spirit of prayer was so intense that the prayer requests spilled over into the afternoon Bible readings. Numbers at the meetings increased and included three 'char-a-banc' [2] loads from as far away as Frinton in Essex. Although people were blessed and sinners were converted, Ipswich was not an easy place to move, and it was not until the last evening—Friday—that the real breakthrough came. At the beginning of the service Douglas Brown stopped the singing of 'Tell Me the Old, Old Story', to remind the congregation of those who had heard Paul and Silas in prison singing at midnight, saying, 'There are people outside Burlington Chapel. I would that they were inside. Often the sermon will fail when the praise of God succeeds.' Douglas Brown had announced that he would go into the school-room where he would see inquirers. As the school-room was separated from the church by a private house it meant that inquirers had to go out into the street, but they were undeterred and a steady stream left the building.

An after-meeting was held in the church under the guidance of Mr. Ferguson and Mr. Parkinson. Speaking to the Convention at Keswick in July, Hugh Ferguson related his experience:

'I shall never forget the after-meeting on the Friday night. When I was appealing to men and women to come to Jesus Christ, to my intense surprise a young woman stepped up on to the lower platform and confessed her love for Jesus Christ; and in a few minutes, one after another, young men and women openly confessed Christ as their personal Saviour.' 3

While preaching in Great Yarmouth the following week, Douglas Brown told the story of that young woman:

'Last Friday night I knelt in a room with a dear girl sixteen years of age. As she knelt at the form she told me her story. She said, 'While you were preaching last night I heard Jesus call me. I ought to have come, but there were two of my friends sitting in the pew and I was frightened to pass them. I could not sleep a wink last night and I have been waiting all day for business to close. I have come tonight and I want to make up for being a coward last night.' I said, 'My dear young friend, what do you want?' She replied, 'I was such a coward last night; I want to face it before all the people.' The schoolroom where we were was two doors higher up the street than the chapel. It was a pouring wet night and I walked back with her to the church. I wanted to stand by her but she did not wait for me. She walked up the three steps on to the platform, turned round and smiled at eleven hundred people. Mr. Ferguson was speaking; he had to stop; and that dear girl looked that congregation in the face and said, "Friends, I love Jesus Christ. I have given my heart to Him".' 4

Some of those who responded that memorable night were so overcome that they burst into tears before they could find words to express them-selves.

Herring Searchers in the North Sea

The Ipswich gatherings only lasted five days but the work of revival was none the less real. Although Douglas Brown returned to London on Saturday morning there were prayer meetings in Ipswich that evening, and again on Monday, 'of great numbers and power', and conversions continued. Mr. Brown returned on Thursday, June 23rd. He was due to preach the annual sermon for the Suffolk Benevolent Society at Stowmarket the following day so a meeting was arranged in Burlington Chapel for Thursday evening. Mr. Parkinson, the minister, was on mission work in West Africa and the Rev. JRM Stephens who was serving in Ipswich for three months, takes up the story:

'It fell to me to preside at the meeting, which was announced for 7.30, but at 7 o'clock the chapel was filling, and by the commencement of the service it was filled to overflowing, over twelve hundred being present. It struck me as very remarkable that on a hot summer evening, with no advertising save the notice board outside bearing the simple announcement of Mr. Brown's return, such a great audience should gather.

The meeting progressed like an ordinary evening service. Mr. Brown preached a heart-searching sermon on Isaiah 44:15-17, showing how man seeks to content himself with the material things of life, and yet remains unsatisfied, too often giving to God the fag-ends and the residue of his days. At the close of a striking message he went into the vestry, having previously intimated that he would be glad to see any who desired to re-consecrate themselves to God, or to surrender themselves to the Lord Jesus Christ. Without delay people passed down the aisle, until some forty three had gone forward. One elderly man hurriedly entered the room and knelt at the table. When he could control his voice he cried, 'A fag-end; I am only a fag-end!' Presently he returned and faced the great congregation, testifying that he had been engaged in Sunday School work for years but not until that night had he realised what was meant by real conversion and commitment to Christ. A young girl of fifteen years of age, led by her father, returned to the chapel smiling happily through her tears, while her mother stayed behind to help three other girls into peace. A woman said that she had been converted in the meetings at Ipswich with five of her brothers and sisters, and her husband had been converted since. Seven adults in one family!' 5

The next day Douglas Brown preached at Stowmarket on 'Divine Sovereignty and Human Responsibility in the Realm of Christian Witness'. It was a message chiefly for ministers and the preacher said, 'When revival comes to England, the sermon-tasters will wither away and will become worshippers. When a man preaches in the power of the Holy Spirit, his message is a miracle of utterance.' Mr. Stephens only attended two meetings but as an observer he was convinced that the movement was of God and under the direction of the Holy Spirit.

'From man's standpoint the results are perplexing. There is hardly any advertising, no sensational methods, and no hysterical appeals—there is only an earnest presentation of God's truth. Though hundreds have been converted, the majority of whom are adults, yet the chief results have been amongst those who are at any rate nominal Christians. They have been brought to a full surrender. The newly won converts too are filled with a spirit of service. One who was brought to Christ at Lowestoft has in the last three months brought fifty others to Him. One great feature of the movement is the resolve of the ministers to shepherd the converts and train them for service; and so make all the existing agencies of the church more fruitful.' [5]

Great Yarmouth, Monday June 5th–Friday June 10th

Douglas Brown's intensive preaching in East Anglia continued throughout the summer of 1921. He left Ipswich on Saturday, preached at Balham on Sunday and began his campaign in Yarmouth on Monday, June 5th. There was close cooperation between the Rev. James Bevan, Vicar of St. George's, the Rev. David John of Park Baptist Chapel and Hugh Ferguson and John Hayes of Lowestoft. On Saturday, June 3rd, a large prayer meeting was held in the Baptist Chapel, conducted by the two Lowestoft ministers. On Sunday James Bevan cycled to Lowestoft to conduct the services at Christ Church while John Hayes preached at St. George's and Hugh Ferguson preached at Park Chapel. A united Bible Class in the Baptist Chapel in the afternoon was led by John Hayes, while at the same time a united service at St. George's was addressed by Hugh Ferguson. After normal evening services Mr. Ferguson, who had cancelled a holiday to help at Yarmouth, preached again at a united evangelistic service at which souls were saved.

The first meeting addressed by Douglas Brown was in Park Baptist Chapel on Monday evening and was extensively reported in the *Eastern Daily News* on Tuesday, June 6th.

'The mission from which a tide of religious revival is expected to sweep through Yarmouth made an excellent start on Monday. Park Baptist Chapel was the scene of the initial evangelistic service, and it was so crowded that tonight's gathering will be held in St. George's Church...

There is plenty of singing of the old favourites of Moody and Sankey, and the hymns go with a swing and volume that is inspiring. There was a crowded church with chairs down the aisles, and the congregation was largely composed of many who are already Christian workers and identified with existing churches of all kinds, both Anglican and Nonconformist.

Mr. Brown said that while he was at Ipswich a request was received for prayer for a godless family, with the result that a father, mother, five sons and two daughters all came out and were converted. 'We have been apologising for the religion of Christ though it should sway everything in this country. We Christians are such cowards; but we have got to come out. Nothing is going to save dear old England but a revival. The nation has turned its back upon God. Oh, that God will bring the church to another Pentecost till she loses all fear. I want you Christians to get the unsaved to these meetings. No one minister is thinking of getting people for his church by this mission... Looking upon this poor tired, dislocated suffering world I can see no other solution than the coming of Christ... You are only going to Heaven by the merits of Christ. It would be a terrible thing if I did not warn men against the wrath to come. There is no easy way to salvation in Yarmouth this week, and the fear of man keeps many away. We have been ashamed of Jesus too long, but He is going to break through and we shall have the happiest week we have ever known.'

During the singing of a hymn Mr. Brown left the pulpit for the vestry and invited inquirers to meet him there. Rev. H Ferguson then took charge of the service, and several persons passed into the inquiry room, while prayers were offered. Mr. Brown returned to the pulpit and the Doxology was sung to close the service, which had lasted for nearly two hours. There is no sensationalism in the style or methods, but undoubtedly a service of this character is a deep emotional experience to all taking part in it.'

The daily routine was the same as it had been at Lowestoft and Ipswich, with a prayer meeting each morning and a Bible reading each afternoon. On Tuesday, and for the rest of the week, the larger St.George's Church was filled beyond its normal capacity of eleven hundred people for the evening meetings. On Wednesday two hundred seats were brought in, while on Thursday and Friday fifteen to sixteen hundred people crowded into the building. People came in from the country and their bicycles were stacked outside the church.

In a newspaper report on Tuesday June 7th, a reporter had asked Douglas Brown, 'Will there be a revival?' He replied that there was revival already when Anglican and Free Church ministers were working hand in hand to secure God's blessing on the town. The report went on to say that he preached with dramatic power on 'The Crucifixion', and young people in twos and fours streamed down the aisle into the inquiry room at the close. This was one of the rare occasions when Douglas Brown indicated that he felt they were in a revival situation.[6] On Wednesday the response was so great that the meeting was closed earlier than usual to allow inquirers to be dealt with, while at the same time a prayer meeting began in the school-room opposite the church. As the huge congregation poured out after a two hour service on Thursday evening they were singing hymns. 'It was a wonderful spectacle,' wrote a reporter.

At the final service on Friday James Bevan, Vicar of St. George's, announced that on Saturday evening there would be a meeting for praise and prayer in Park Baptist Chapel. He also said that the great gathering reminded him of what he had seen in the Welsh revival. In his address Mr. Brown said that this was the last service of a week of Pentecost. He went on: 'This is my three hundred and fiftieth service since March 7th, and I have been asking God that three hundred and fifty people in Yarmouth may give their hearts to him.' Taking as his text the well-known verse, 'Present your bodies a living sacrifice,' he pleaded, 'Surrender of self is the way of salvation...I don't want you to be driven along by excitement but broken by the love of God, bowed with shame that you have never answered the claim of Calvary before.' During the week hundreds had indicated their commitment to Jesus Christ.

At Norwich two weeks later Douglas Brown related the following story of conversion:

'After the sermon in St. George's Church Yarmouth there came an old man of seventy eight. He had had visions of Christ when he was a young man and used to go out preaching locally. Then he discovered that he was a professor, not a possessor, and instead of confessing it to his Lord he gave up Christian work. He had said that he would at least be honest if he could not be holy; but he had never come to Jesus and started again. So the years had drifted by. He had then been only thirty-odd years of age, today he is seventy eight. He came into St. George's Church that night, and as he listened to the gospel God's Holy Spirit moved on the face of old age and laid His hand on the shoulder of the old patriarch without Christ, and he rose. I can see him now as he came down the aisle and passed through that curtain by the pulpit. I wish I was an artist; I'd like to paint that picture and put the text beneath it, as that poor withered, aged arm rested on the forehead, and the white locks rested against the wall of the church, and the tears streamed down the long beard, and the old frame shook. We knelt together, and God brought him home before the clock struck midnight, and restored unto him "the years the locust had eaten".' [6]

Norwich, Monday June 27th - Friday July 1st

Two weeks after concluding at Yarmouth, Douglas Brown commenced a week of meetings in Norwich. Hugh Ferguson described them as unforgettable: 'Every building that we had for the evening services was packed with men and women, many of whom found Christ'. The visit, like those to other places, was given very little publicity; only a brief notice in the local press. A clergyman came to Norwich and asked a railway porter the shortest way to the cathedral. 'The Rev. Douglas Brown is preaching here,' was the reply, 'and if you want a good thing I would advise you to leave the cathedral alone and go down to St. Mary's Chapel. I have been there every night and I have got what is well worth getting, and if you want a good thing that is the place to go.' That is how the meetings were publicised.

St. Mary's Baptist Chapel was crowded to capacity for the opening service, with extra chairs placed down the aisles. The first hymn was 'Rescue the Perishing', and it was interrupted by Douglas Brown who appealed to believers in the congregation to go to the school-room and pray, and so make room for those who were crowding around the doors to come in. It was striking that Douglas Brown was accompanied in the pulpit by Canon Hay Aitken, Canon Residentiary of Norwich Cathedral. Converted in the 1859 revival, his formerly raven hair and beard now white, he looked an impressive figure as he stood in the pulpit and prayed extemporarily with great fervour. Before reading the Scriptures Mr. Brown said:

'I have come to Norwich because I believe it is the will of God that I should spend this week with you... I ask you to pray earnestly in your homes that there may be poured upon this city a spirit of conviction of sin. Until men and women realise themselves to be sinners in God's sight, there will be no receiving of the word of God unto salvation. Brothers and sisters, nothing will save our beloved land but a revival from heaven... O God, this week send forth Thy Holy Spirit and purge the churches. Bring back backsliders, give a great sense of sin, answer mothers' prayers, fathers' prayers, for children; answer children's prayers for parents. Whatever there may be wrong in any church, O God, put it right this week. Let it be known in this city that God is at work; let it be a week of great rejoicing, as we stand still and see the salvation of the Lord! Pray earnestly. You cannot make a revival; but no multitude of people ever got down on its knees before Calvary but what revival came. God bring us back to Calvary, back to that dear old Gospel in all its simplicity. May the pierced hands of Jesus Christ rescue hundreds of souls this week. See to it that you pray. Pray in the Holy Spirit, and God will answer with miracles of grace.'[6]

This was probably a spontaneous expression of Douglas Brown's desire and prayer. It shows his uncomplicated concept of revival and the central place he gave to the Gospel and the cross in his preaching.

After reading from Matthew's Gospel the account of Jesus and Peter walking on the water, Douglas Brown preached, and this is how the local press reporter described him: 'With out-spread and uplifted hands employed in gestures never inappropriate though possibly a little too profuse, he declared that nothing will save our beloved nation but a revival from heaven, for we had turned our backs upon God. With a fine modulated voice, sometimes breaking with emotion and sometimes rising in appeal almost to the level of a command, he uttered a typical evangelistic address, doctrinally of the sort that might have fallen forty years ago from DL Moody.'

After preaching, Douglas Brown went to the vestry to talk with those who were anxious about their souls, while Hugh Ferguson addressed waverers 'in grave and measured words of appeal', to which a number responded. During the hymn which followed, the singing was stopped to allow Canon Hay Aitken to speak to the undecided and to urge upon people the importance of confessing Christ with the words, 'If thou shalt confess with thy mouth Jesus as Lord, and believe in thine heart that God raised Him from the dead, thou shalt be saved.' (Romans 10:9)

On Tuesday evening, Princes Street Congregational Church was crowded to capacity. Before preaching Douglas Brown commented on the lack of any formal programme of meetings in the different places he visited. 'For four long months I have been watching for the salvation of the Lord without any programme. If you had met with an organised committee of clergy and ministers to consider the possibility of a week's mission in the city of Norwich in a broiling week at the end of June, do you think it would ever have happened?' There were so many seekers at the close that Hugh Ferguson, who was in charge of the meeting, asked his fellow ministers on the platform to go to the inquiry room, 'where many anxious inquirers are waiting for someone to speak to them about their souls' salvation.'

A report in *The Christian* by the Rev. Sydney Laver of Chapel-in-the-Field Congregational Church, claimed that the revival in East Anglia had reached Norwich. He wrote that it had at least four distinctive features: spontaneity, togetherness, prayer and the Spirit of Witness. He was amazed at the courage of some young Christians. As in other places, the prayer meetings had been in the mornings, with local young people pleading for the salvation of their parents and grand-parents, together with prayer requests from all over the country. Three of the largest churches in the city were packed on successive evenings and twice there were overflow meetings. Although many converts had been gathered in, Mr. Laver felt the greatest work had been done among Christians.

A fortnight later Douglas Brown returned to Norwich to preach at Chapel-in-the-Field Congregational Church. Although it was midweek during a spell of very hot weather, the church was well filled in the afternoon and crammed in the evening. Mr. Brown was suffering from blood-poisoning of the leg and medical opinion had advised a rest. In the afternoon he preached on Lamentations 3:51 'Mine eye affecteth mine heart'. Although more than once he remarked that he 'must go on slowly', the press report said there were passages in his pleading during which 'the preacher flashed forth with his accustomed fire'. In the evening the seating capacity was taxed to the utmost. The service was conducted by Fred Humphrey of St. Mary's Baptist Church and, in spite of the soaring temperature, Douglas Brown seemed to forget his disability. He preached with great power on the links between the Old Testament picture of the three anointings of David, and the three appearings of the Lord Jesus Christ.

There were remarkable instances of conversion at Norwich. Three engaged couples were at one of the services and each of the three young women went to the inquiry room, accepted Christ and resolved to tell their young men immediately, what had happened to them. They found that all three young men had come under conviction, had gone to another inquiry room and had been converted themselves. A husband and wife, who were not Christians, went to the meeting in Princes Street Congregational Church. The lady went to the inquiry room, accepted Christ, then went to confess her new-found faith to her husband, only to find that he had also been converted. Four young fellows from an outlying village came into a church in Norwich where a meeting was being held, to see and hear for themselves. Nothing was further from their minds than that they would be converted, but they were—all four of them! Canon Hay Aitken made the following observation to *The Christian*:

'Mr. Brown preaches the old gospel with simplicity and directness, and there can be no question as to his earnestness and yearning love for souls. His style is much less anecdotal than was that of DL Moody, and that makes his hold on the people all the more remarkable. It was delightful to see clergymen and ministers working together in the inquiry room, and took one's mind back to the dear old days gone by, when that was no uncommon sight.' 7

Cambridge, Monday July 11th - Friday July 15th

At Cambridge the meetings were held in Zion Baptist Church in tropical weather. Advertising was meagre, with a single poster over the church door and a few small hand-bills and some notices distributed in the churches on the Sunday. There was no committee and no organisation, but working with Douglas Brown were the Baptist Minister, Rev. Edward Milnes, the Rev. E Church, Vicar of St. Andrew-the-Less, and the Superintendent Minister of the Primitive Methodists, the Rev. J Rose. Also assisting at these meetings in his own home town was the well-known evangelist, Gipsy Smith. Prayer meetings were held in the mornings with large numbers of requests, as in previous missions. The prayer meetings and Bible addresses were all well attended, and the evening gospel services were crowded. Among the themes taken up by the preacher in the evenings were 'Christ in the Barrack-room' and 'The Common Salvation'.

At one of the mission services, Douglas Brown interrupted the singing of the hymn after the sermon and said, 'I want you to be silent and be seated. I am quite sure a battle is raging within some of you. You say to yourself, 'I want to be a Christian, I want to come to Jesus, I know I ought to do that but I fear to come down the aisle'. Well, if Jesus Christ isn't worth walking down the aisle for, He isn't worth having. Now, I want all the Christians in this building just to give themselves to prayer. While they are praying, I am going to walk up the aisle, and while I plead with men and women in different parts of the building, Christians get to work and pray, and if anyone is sitting next to you under conviction of sin, come along with them. O God, bring back courage to the Christian Church! I am going to take that journey which you are dreading. It is a lovely journey when you take it for Christ's sake.' He then walked in the aisles of the church reciting gospel invitations and scripture promises. When he returned to the front, Douglas Brown made a final appeal. He said it had been a lovely journey and appealed to others to take it, 'and together let us kneel and hand over our lives to Jesus.'

In the five days of the mission in Cambridge some two hundred people were dealt with in the inquiry rooms and there were remarkable instances of conversion. A woman of advanced years was converted at one of the meetings and told her story. She had been brought under conviction of sin through the preaching of Gipsy Smith years before, but had held back from yielding her life to Jesus Christ. From that day she began to pass through a series of distressing experiences. Reading of Douglas Brown's meetings in Cambridge she had travelled from her home in Nottingham to hear him, in the hope, (as she put it), 'that God would call again.' After hearing the message, she struggled for half an hour before entering into the peace of believing. Douglas Brown also told of two people from a village ten miles out of Cambridge who came to one meeting, where they were moved by the Holy Spirit to re-dedicate their lives to God. Returning home they gathered a prayer meeting together in the village, and the next evening brought two others to the meeting, who were both soundly converted.

In a sermon at Cambridge Douglas Brown told how he was preaching on the subject of surrender to Christ, when a man came into the vestry and said, 'Sir, a quarter of an hour ago I felt as if I could go into the pulpit and knock you down, but then God's Spirit knocked me down. I have been an officer in the church for years, but I have not been a Christian.' He went back into the after-meeting and told everyone, 'Friends, I have been a Christian worker for ten years, but I have only been a Christian for two minutes.' The preacher also gave two personal reminiscences while at Cambridge. He told of when he was a boy and Charles Haddon Spurgeon was his 'great big friend'. He went on, 'Mr. Spurgeon was a great man who

Christ Church and the Beach Village, Lowestoft, as it was in 1921

had great power with men because he had a big Jesus Christ. He lost himself in Jesus, he just preached Christ and in some wonderful way that big Christ seemed to catch up His little servant and invest him with spiritual greatness.' Douglas Brown used this to stress the importance of those who were working for Christ in the villages.

On another occasion while at Cambridge he related how his sister Nellie was the means of his conversion when he was a boy of seven. His father had called him into his study one Monday morning and told him how he had heard cries from Nellie's bedroom the previous evening: 'Jesus, win the battle for me.' Archibald Brown had been preaching on, 'Who will go for us? Whom shall I send?' and the reply, 'Here am I, send me.' A little while later the voice broke out again, 'Lord Jesus I see it! I'll never have peace till you are my Master! I'm willing to go.' Later, Nellie went out to China with the China Inland Mission. All this made a profound impression upon young Douglas, so much so that he always said that Nellie had won him for

Jesus Christ and was, therefore, linked with everyone converted through his preaching in East Anglia.

Gipsy Smith commented on the meetings at Cambridge in *The Christian:*

'The Rev. Douglas Brown is in Cambridge, my home town, conducting services in Zion Baptist Church. I have had the joy of being present and wish to bear this witness. He is a chosen vessel. God is with him, and the message comes like a 'thus saith the Lord'. He has been thrust out—that is the word, THRUST OUT—by the Holy Ghost, with his message to the churches of our dear land. I do most earnestly ask my brethren to listen to the voice of God through him, and to be willing in the day of God's power. It may be our day of visitation. The Lord is with our dear brother. My heart bows before the power of God manifested in and through him, and my prayer will follow him.' [8]

At the final meeting in Cambridge, Douglas Brown and Gipsy Smith 'clasped hands with their faces all aglow', and at the close about thirty responded to a powerful appeal.

Revival and convention

The autumn of 1921 proved to be as momentous as the spring in parts of East Anglia, as the Spirit of God continued to work powerfully, especially at the Convention in Lowestoft and amongst the Scottish fisherfolk at Great Yarmouth. Early in September Douglas Brown gave his appraisal of the spiritual climate in the nation as a whole, and in East Anglia in particular:

'A momentous revival is within the reach of the churches. In East Anglia it has commenced. Whether it becomes national depends upon the message and methods adopted by various churches during the coming winter. You cannot organise a revival any more than setting off maroons [9] on Hampstead Heath would break up the recent drought. The army of organised religion is a great host. The possibilities are immense. But the great machine is hung up and powerless for want of water. When critics stop picking holes in Divine revelation, when cranks cease to prejudice others by religious squint, when preachers cease to be politicians, when churches put spiritual before social, when Calvary preaching replaces critical essays, when God's atmosphere impregnates man's activity, when pride, jealousy, gossip and worldliness wither and die in our churches under the blazing heat of a Calvary love, then the churches will strike the rock of salvation with Divine authority, and the waters will flow for the healing of the nations.' [10]

The report also stated that Mr. Brown would take part in the Lowestoft Convention, then travel to Southampton on October 6th before re-visiting Great Yarmouth, Ipswich, Norwich and Cambridge.

The Lowestoft Convention for the deepening of spiritual life was held from Monday, September 19th to Friday, September 23rd. As well as Douglas Brown there were speakers from the Keswick Convention—Mr. W B Sloan, the Rev. EL Langston and the Rev. FW Ainley. Christ Church was full to overflowing for the opening meeting, and in his address Mr. Sloan said that central to all their messages would be 'Jesus Christ and Him crucified'. The Rev. EL Langston said he felt it would not be an ordinary convention because tens of thousands of prayers were being offered all over the country for Lowestoft that week. The pattern of the meetings was the same as it had been throughout the time of revival earlier in the year, with prayer meetings in the mornings, Bible readings in the afternoons and convention meetings in the evenings.

At one of the evening meetings at Christ Church, the Rev. FW Ainley told how, while he was in Jamaica, he saw a spider throw its web around a fire-fly, extinguishing its glow. It happened in the study of a Christian doctor who broke the spider's web and set the fire-fly free to fly and glow again. When he preached at that same meeting, Douglas Brown saw the incident as an analogy of Christians who were bound and whose light was almost extinguished and who needed to be set free. Whether the preacher knew about this incident before the meeting, or whether he abandoned his prepared message is not clear, but it was certainly an example of how he was inspired and led by the Spirit of God, and it had a powerful effect upon the congregation.

On another evening, Douglas Brown preached on 'The Secret of Revival' and gave personal testimony to God's dealings with him, and to what he described as his 'baptism of the Holy Ghost' before his first coming to Lowestoft in March:

'I confess with sorrow and shame, humbly before God that the last eight months of my life have been months of tremendous emptying. Blessed be God! they have been months of filling. I am giving this little bit of experience humbly to the glory of God, that it may help others. I only really learned the meaning of the baptism of the Holy Ghost at the end of last February, and I had been a minister of Jesus Christ for twenty seven years. I thank God for that morning when He nearly broke my heart in my study, when I saw all the things that were wrong, and I knew that the only hope of usefulness and power, and joy, and gentleness, and love, was for Jesus Christ to come into my life and absolutely reign; and He showed me that just as I had received a Saviour by an act of faith, so I had to come humbly and penitently to His feet and receive the gift of the Holy Ghost.

I can remember that morning as if it were this morning. As I knelt there with the tears running down my cheeks, I said, "Lord Jesus, I am not worthy. I feel I ought not to ask for such a thing. Thou mightest strike me dead for presumption; but, O Jesus, Thou hast told me, Thou hast led me, Thou hast brought me to this. For the sake of my church, for the sake of my congregation, for the sake of the men and women that I meet day by day, for the sake of my witness to that wonderful Calvary, Lord Jesus, I trust Thee, I ask Thee now to give me the Holy Spirit. I would receive Him for a life of purity, a life of power, a life of loyalty to Jesus, a life of faithful witness. None of these things could ever be mine in my own power. I am a horrible failure, and I know it! O Lord, give me Thy Holy Spirit," and He led me, He gave me fire that morning, and I thanked Jesus Christ. I did not think about my failings. I never felt so bad in my life, but I took Him. Within four days I was in Lowestoft; the cloud burst, and souls were being born again by the score.'[11]

It was reported in *The Lowestoft Journal* that there were thanksgiving services in Christ Church and in the Congregational Church on the Friday evening. Douglas Brown spoke at both services and a report of his address at the former was given in *The Christian Herald*: 'Well beforehand Christ Church was full, and after some hymn-singing the service was conducted by the Vicar, the Rev. John Hayes, while the Rev. WG Hardie, Vicar of St. John's, led the prayers. Mr. Sloan delivered a devotional address and then Mr. Brown spoke of the wonderful results of the week. He said that the predominant feature had been the 'felt presence of Christ', and that in Lowestoft God had brought Convention and Revival together. In conclusion Mr. Brown asked everyone who had received definite help and blessing in the meetings to stand in silent thanksgiving, and the large congregation rose with one accord.' [12]

In his address in the Congregational Church entitled 'Revival and What Should Follow', Douglas Brown again brought Convention and Revival together:

'Now it has pleased Almighty God that this new flood of religious consciousness that has come into existence, should commence its outflow in East Anglia, and of all the meetings that I have ever attended—and I have attended meetings in all parts of the world—I have never been at a series of meetings more wonderful than these meetings that come to a close this evening. I want God the Holy Spirit on this last evening to lead us into spiritual understanding of these great experiences through which, by His grace and His love, He has allowed you and me to pass. Have you noticed that there has been a wonderful combination of spiritual experience and spiritual activity this week?

The Convention has been with us all the week, and we praise God for it. The Revival has been with us all the week, and I think some of us have learnt what we never learnt before....Sins have been dealt with and sinners converted every day, and none of us has said, "This Convention has been spoilt", rather all God's people have said, "This is what we have been praying and longing for." And after all friends, isn't it the normal condition of the true knowledge of Jesus Christ that saints shall be so in touch with their Master, and so absolutely mastered by the message of the Cross of Christ, that it shall lay this constraint upon them, under the inspiration of the Gospel, that it is not alone for us, to stretch out a loving hand and to plead with others to come under the canopy of the Redeeming Cross and find salvation for their souls? I thank God that this week there have been kneeling together in the church those who have been seeking a personal Saviour, and those to whom the Spirit of God has shown the sin of backsliding, and under His blessed ministry have been brought into full surrender to the will of God.' [13]

Thus, the first and most notable convention in Lowestoft came to a close. It seemed to be a continuation of the days of revival that had begun in March, and the hearts of many were longing that the work of revival which began in Lowestoft and other parts of East Anglia then, would not only continue there, but would also spread throughout the land.

When Scotland comes to Yarmouth

As the convention was closing in Lowestoft, thousands of Scottish fisherfolk were beginning the long journey south by sea and land to Lowestoft and Great Yarmouth for the herring season. Following the shoals of herring, in the first months of the year the fishermen worked from Stornoway on Lewis, then from April to June they moved to the Shetland Isles, and from June to September they went on to fishing grounds accessible from Wick, parts of the Moray Firth, Fraserburgh and Peterhead. In the autumn they moved down to the East Anglian ports. The boats with their crews of nine or ten would head south, and the fisher-girls, including wives, sweethearts and sisters who would gut the herring for curing, made the long journey by train. It had been a poor season in the north, but hopes were high as the boats and trains made their way south. As they arrived at Lowestoft the boats were met by the Baptist Minister, the Rev. Hugh Ferguson, who welcomed their crews as a fellow Scotsman. Unlike the local boats the Scottish fleet would not put to sea on Sundays, and with all the boats in harbour scores of their crewmen in their caps and jerseys would make their way to the Baptist Church, Brethren Assemblies and other missions in the town. A similar picture could be found at Yarmouth, with congregations being swelled in the Brethren Hall, Park Baptist Tabernacle, Deneside Methodist Church and the Salvation Army Citadel. It was in such a setting that God moved in great power again.

Troup, the converted cooper

Douglas Brown was still preaching in different parts of East Anglia during the autumn of 1921 and was at hand when revival broke out amongst the fisherfolk. In His sovereign purpose, God introduced another instrument into the work of revival at this time; this was Jock Troup, a cooper or barrel-maker, who came down from Wick, on the east coast of Caithness, to work in the fish-curing yards at Yarmouth. Jock was born

Scottish girls gutting herrings, Lowestoft

at Dallachie on the Moray Firth in 1896, and when he was seven his family moved to Wick, which was then the premier fishing port in Scotland. Although he was brought up in a Christian home by praying parents, Jock did not respond to the gospel when he was young. He left school and worked as an apprentice cooper. He became very skilled, but the work was hard and the hours were long and his own time was spent in seeking pleasure. Jock Troup was in trouble with the local magistrates, he fell over a railway bridge, and twice he was rescued from drowning. By the grace of God this wayward young man became His instrument in revival at Yarmouth and in Scotland. Later, Jock Troup became superintendent of the famous Tent Hall in Glasgow, and an evangelist on both sides of the Atlantic.

It was on board ship in Kingston harbour near Dublin that Jock Troup was converted, while serving in the Royal Naval Patrol Service during the

North Sea Gateway

First World War. A godly couple, Mr. and Mrs. West, regularly conducted a gospel meeting each Sunday evening in the YMCA hall in Dublin, and after listening to the preaching on one occasion, Jock cheerfully said to Mr. West, 'I think I'll get converted.' He goes on to describe his experience:

'Little did I think that God would take me at my word. Something laid hold on my life and I became utterly miserable. I tried to throw it off but the conviction deepened. We left for patrol the next day, Monday, and I could never explain the awful misery of that week. Day and night I was like a hunted man; my sin was before me every moment. I tried to get rid of it by resolving to turn over a new leaf, but it seemed the more I tried, the more my conscience smote me. I stopped swearing and gambling and tried to give up smoking. When none of these things could give me peace, I made up my mind that I would go and speak to Mr. West whenever our time of patrol finished.

The burden had grown till it kept me from sleeping lest I should die and wake up in hell. How faithfully my wife dealt with me by showing me from the Scriptures what Christ had accomplished on my behalf! I listened to it all but could not grasp the wonderful truth of it. She then prayed for me and got others to pray for me, but it seemed to me that I was beyond hope. I left the building feeling like one of the damned.

On arriving at the ship however, I opened the wheel house door and got on my knees and cried to God to save me for Jesus' sake. My burden simply rolled away and the deliverance was so sweet that I rushed into the cabin to tell the crew what had happened. The cards were on the table as usual and the members of the crew were awaiting my return to have a hand. What a shock when I told them I was saved! Some mocked and gave me a few days to hold out,—but praise God He has led me on.' [1]

After the war Jock Troup returned to his home town of Wick and resumed his occupation making barrels. He also served God by attaching himself to the Salvation Army and preaching the gospel at every opportunity. In 1920, while in Aberdeen, Jock had dealings with God which affected the whole of his future life and ministry. In his short biography, *Our Beloved Jock*, James Alexander Stewart DD describes his experience in an appendix entitled, *The Secret:*

'Mrs. Troup has reminded me that the secret of all her husband's ministry was the mighty experience that took place in 1920 in the Fishermen's Mission at Aberdeen. Something glorious happened there that made him the man he became. He entered into a definite experience with the blessed Holy Spirit. This experience was so sacred to him that he did not mention it often, and then only to a few intimate friends. I am sure that our beloved brother would have called it 'a baptism of power for service'. In Bible conferences and revival rallies I have heard him again and again emphasise his belief that every Christian must have a definite dealing with the Holy Spirit for an effective witness for Christ. One of his favourite verses was: 'But ye shall receive power after that the Holy Ghost is come upon you: and ye shall be witnesses unto me both in Jerusalem, and in all Judea, and in Samaria, and unto the uttermost part of the earth.' (Acts 1:8)

It was against this background that Jock Troup arrived at Yarmouth in the autumn of 1921.

Saturday was always a big day for the Scottish fisherfolk during the East Anglian herring season, because they would come in with their catches and not put to sea again until Monday. Throughout Saturday morning the girls would pack the fish ready for market and then they would all be free for shopping in the afternoon, followed by a happy get-together on Saturday evening. Jock Troup seized the opportunity to preach the gospel in the Market Place after the stalls had closed. On the third Saturday in October, at about nine o'clock, he opened his Bible at Isaiah 63:1 and began to preach, 'Who is this that cometh from Edom, with dyed garments from Bozrah? This that is glorious in his apparel? I that speak in righteousness, mighty to save.' Suddenly the power of God came down, as it had done in revivals before, and strong fishermen were thrown to the ground and cried to God for mercy. One man who was there said that he was literally 'slain of the Lord' and fell to the ground; others did the same; he described it as being like a battlefield. Later, in Eyemouth in north Scotland, after the fishermen had returned home, a Methodist local preacher said he was one of the first to 'fall' at Yarmouth. The flood-gates were opened that Saturday evening and in the next few weeks hundreds were saved.

The movement that began so dramatically continued day after day as people were brought under deep conviction of sin, irresistibly drawn to Christ and completely transformed. Sometimes the fisher-girls were too distressed to continue work and Jock Troup had to be sent for to counsel them. On one occasion three girls failed to turn up at the curing yard on Monday morning and their employer found them still in their lodgings deeply troubled in their souls. Jock was sent for. He led them to Christ and they happily returned to their work.

The story is told of Alex Thain from Port Gordon, who was walking past the Market Place one Saturday night with five of his friends when suddenly he found himself standing alone because his friends had yielded to the call of Christ. Being attached to the Salvation Army, Jock Troup was used to open-air preaching and converts would kneel in the ring on the pavement in response to his appeals. James Slater, fisherman, writer and poet from Portsoy in Banffshire, told of outstanding trophies of grace from the gospel preaching with men being changed from heavy drinkers to hymn-singing, Bible-loving Christians; one being his father-in-law, Jack (Tartan) Pirie.

Men were saved out on the sea at the fishing grounds off Happisburgh, Norfolk, and in an area of sea known as Smith's Knoll. The father of Jackie Ritchie, author of *Floods on Dry Ground* which is an account of the revival among the Scottish fisherfolk, was converted in that way. A telegram home from another Ritchie (Bobby) read, 'Saved ten miles from Knoll Lightship. Last to ring in on this ship.' By November it became clear that the herring season would be one of the worst on record, mainly due to the severe weather which included gales and snow. Unable to put to sea the crews were free to attend meetings during the week, both in and out of doors, and although the harvest of the sea was sparse there was a rich harvest of souls.

'The Divil's...rare bad time'

Douglas Brown returned to Yarmouth for the first two weeks of November, and for a short time he and Jock Troup joined forces in preaching the gospel. Evening meetings were held in Deneside Methodist Church and in St. George's Church. On one occasion the cultured Baptist minister and the rough herring cooper were together in the pulpit of the Deneside Church, weeping over the lost and in over-flowing love to the Saviour at the same time.

In November the revival ministry in Yarmouth passed from Jock Troup to Douglas Brown when the former was suddenly removed from the scene. Whether or not Jock's preaching, and particularly his counselling the distressed, disrupted his work as a cooper, he was dismissed from his employment and took it as a message from God that he was to give himself wholly to the work of the gospel. At the same time he had a vision of a man praying in Fraserburgh that God would send to them the evangelist He was using in Yarmouth. After confiding to a few friends what God had so clearly shown him, Jock left for the north, to the surprise of many. *The Yarmouth and Gorleston Times* gave a sympathetic account of Jock Troup and his work there:

'Jock is an excellent advertisement for Christianity. There is a heartiness about his 'Amens' and 'Hallelujahs' that makes people believe he has got something worth having. "Some people call me mad," said Jock. "There's goin to be many more mad in Yarmouth afore this week is over. What will the ould divil be thinkin' noo I wonder? I bet he's havin' a rare bad time." Every evening, and three times on Sundays, he has held open-air meetings in the Market Place or on the Hall Quay. Many converts kneel down in the street each night.' [2]

Revival among the fisherfolk continued in Yarmouth under the preaching of Douglas Brown. A large number of workers were drawn in for what *The Christian Herald* called 'Yarmouth's wonderful ten days'. The Rev. Philip Rogers, a Congregationalist, came from Cardiff, and another Welshman, the Rev. DJ Hiley who was a Baptist minister in Norwood, arrived about the same time. Six students came from Spurgeon's College, and ministers from Yarmouth and Lowestoft also helped, together with the Salvation Army, Quakers and Plymouth Brethren. In addition, from among the fishermen themselves there were men preaching, like Bill Bruce and David Cordiner, of whom much was to be heard when they returned to Scotland. Meetings were held in four churches. In the mornings the body of the Congregational Church was filled for prayer meetings, Bible expositions were given in the Deneside Wesleyan Church in the afternoons, and the evening evangelistic meetings were held in both St. George's and Deneside Churches, with Regent Road Primitive Methodist Church often being used to accommodate the overflow. At the morning prayer meetings there were no hymns or sermon but only intercession. Some two hundred requests for prayer poured in every day. Prayers were not more than a minute long and they were for relatives, friends, backsliders, shipmates and fellow-workers. As the days went by the prayers were interspersed with cries of 'Glory!' as the answers were noted and the requests put on one side. Each afternoon around seven hundred people would make their way to the Deneside Wesleyan Church, through blizzards, hurricane-force winds and flying debris, to hear the Word of God. In the evenings there were the evangelistic meeetings, which were later described by Mr. Brown when preaching at a church in London:

'The services were timed for 7.30, but by 6.30 the people had gathered for singing and prayer, and by 7.30 both St George's and Deneside Wesleyan Church were filled to suffocation, many standing in the aisles and sitting on the window-sills, each gathering numbering at least fifteen hundred people. And they would stay till ten o'clock or half past. The last night I was there I left the church at eleven o'clock, and they were singing then! I did not get home even then, for on my way I came across a batch of young fellows seeking salvation and, though it was raining hard, I stayed to point them to Jesus.'3

Douglas Brown went on to describe what he considered the most notable meeting of his Yarmouth mission. It was a prayer meeting on the evening of November 5th which was attended by fifteen hundred people.

'We started at six o'clock and went on until eleven. No-one was asked to pray but it was all prayer. The power of God was so terrific that we ministers on the platform could do nothing as those dear Scottish fellows prayed. I shall never forget the scene, nor recover from the sense of God's presence at that meeting. The fisher-lads prayed for their brothers; the fisher-girls prayed for the other girls lodging in the same house. Singing, sobs and prayer prevailed in all parts of the building.

After a while we thought it would be good to have testimonies. When Jesus is really in a place and there is a sense of sin and a vision of Calvary, the atmosphere is so gentle, so pure, that a few soft words only were needed to ask for testimonies. I will shut my eyes and picture the scene. Up gets a man from Stornoway and says in his Scottish accent, 'Let's have number 46.' In a moment the Scots girls had taken up the old metre and the place was ringing with 'He drew me out of the horrible pit'. And as those lasses sang, and the strong hefty fishermen joined in, many of them sank down on their knees. Then a lad got up and said, 'I gave myself to God in the fish market last week, and it has been the best week I ever had!' A lassie followed saying, 'I gave my heart to Jesus Christ last night, and my soul is full of laughter!' Another man said, 'I came to Him, Sir, on Tuesday, and He has saved me marvellously.' Then a crowd of them broke out singing:

'Tis done , the great transaction's done;
I am my Lord's, and He is mine!'

I tell you frankly, if a man could pass through a meeting like that without breaking his heart with joy, he must be made of granite.' 4

Open air meetings were going on each day in spite of blizzard conditions and on Saturday night, November 6th, between eleven o'clock and midnight, in a howling gale and torrential rain, twenty two men went down on their knees in the wet and committed themselves to Christ. And that was after a prayer meeting that had lasted four hours! When Douglas Brown returned to his hotel that night, he heard above the gale, 'Hallelujah for the Cross', as singing converts tramped along the main street.

As in other preaching missions, there were remarkable stories of conversion during Douglas Brown's visit to Yarmouth that memorable autumn. A man who lived in a village about twenty miles from John o'Groats, saw a report of Douglas Brown's missions in the press, read one of his sermons and came under conviction of sin. He told his wife he knew he was a sinner, and he had no rest day or night for six weeks. His doctor advised him to go and see Mr. Brown, so he travelled from John o'Groats, arriving at Yarmouth at six o'clock on Monday morning. He went to the meeting in Deneside Wesleyan Church that same afternoon and was the first to respond to the appeal, shouting 'I'm saved, I'm saved!' The convert was anxious to return home to make up for the time he had not been able to work because of his distressed condition, and also to witness to his two boys, who both soon came to the Saviour.

There were three fishermen from one family on a trawler and the younger son insulted his father, who was the skipper, for which he was beaten up by his older brother. The young fellow was so upset that he tried to commit suicide and threw himself into the harbour. A rope was thrown to him and he was rescued. The next day he was drawn into St. George's Church by the sound of singing. His elder brother was there, so was his father, and at the close all three came to Christ. That was three out of a crew of ten converted, whereupon the skipper requested prayer for the others, and by the end of the week the whole crew had been saved.

An evangelist who was trained at the same college as Douglas Brown, but who had gone back after fifteen years and who was at this time broken and ashamed, was restored under his preaching. One evening in St. George's Church a young Scottish fisherman came down the aisle accompanied by a well-dressed young lady. After they had both knelt briefly at the communion rail, the young fellow got up, stepped back and clasped his hands in prayer. The Vicar approached him and asked if he was a friend of the girl. 'I never saw her before,' he replied. 'I came to Jesus last night; I could see that she wanted Him and nobody went to her, so I invited her to come with me.' At the close of the service the young man escorted her down the aisle again and took her to her seat. On the morning Douglas Brown left

Yarmouth, another young woman was on the station platform waiting for him. She had spent a sleepless night under conviction of sin and there and then before the train left she was led to the Saviour.

One of the worst herring seasons on record came to an end. The Scottish boats prepared for home and set their courses northward. The shore workers left by train after the boats had sailed. It was an armada that left Yarmouth and Lowestoft and sailed up the east coast. The boats for Eyemouth and ports on the Firth of Forth and the Firth of Tay turned off first. Next it was the Peterhead vessels, and then those going further west to the ports along the Moray Firth. Others continued north to Wick. News of a mighty movement of God's Spirit at Yarmouth and Lowestoft had filtered through to the communities to which the boats and trains returned. Families were eagerly awaiting loved ones who had been transformed by the grace of God in one of the most powerful movements of the Holy Spirit in a momentous year. Although the blessing was poured out in an East Anglian fishing town, it had far-reaching results in many similar communities along the north-east coast of Scotland. Lowestoft, where the work of revival had begun in March, was touched again, and received a spiritual uplift from the annual visit of the Scottish fishermen for many years afterwards.

Both in March and in November 1921, the movement had three simple ingredients, praying, preaching and singing. Hundreds had participated in the prayer meetings. There were two preachers, one cultured and the other comparatively unlettered, but both with lips touched by a live coal from God's altar. The hymn singing that had been so prominent in the spring and summer came to the fore again, with metrical psalms, Moody and Sankey hymns about the cross, and sacred songs with the tang of the sea about them, all sung with tremendous fervour. People who heard the preaching and participated in the praying and singing never forgot it, and more than fifty years afterwards could speak about it as though it happened yesterday.

The Scottish Dimension

In response to his strong conviction and a clear vision, Jock Troup left Yarmouth for Fraserburgh in November 1921. It was said that by the time his train reached Crewe, he had led to Christ all the other people in the compartment! On arrival in Fraserburgh Jock went to the Market Place and began to preach the gospel. Although it was a cold and windy night, a crowd soon gathered and listened attentively to the rugged preacher. 'Why not go to the Baptist Church?' suggested someone when he had finished. 'I don't know where it is,' Jock replied. He was immediately led to the church, accompanied by many of his hearers. They arrived just as the Pastor, the Rev. W Gilmour, and the Deacons were leaving after a meeting at which they had decided to write to Jock Troup to urge him to come to Fraserburgh! Among the Deacons was the very man whom Jock Troup had seen praying in the vision he had received in Yarmouth. They all went back into the church and, encouraged by the Pastor, Jock went up on the platform and started to lead a meeting. He had only just commenced with a few choruses when people began weeping over their lost condition and seeking the Saviour. The revival had spread to Scotland.

There are other accounts of the revival in north-east Scotland in 1921 and the years following, but its close connection with the movement in Yarmouth and Lowestoft brings it within the scope of this story. It also shows a clear example of Divine strategy. The revival north of the border originated in East Anglia because, although God had already been at work along the north-east coast before the fishing fleet left to follow the herring southward, as they did each autumn, it was when the crews and shore workers returned home that the mercy drops became abundant showers.

Captain William Leed of the Salvation Army described the connection between the work in East Anglia and north-east Scotland as 'The Strategy of God':

'Surely Divine strategy arranged three independent spiritual spearheads to simultaneously attack East Anglia in 1921 with wide reaching results. The Rev. Douglas Brown

Herring drifters putting to sea

was mightily used in Lowestoft and the surrounding area; in Yarmouth, Jock Troup, the Scottish evangelist, then a Salvationist, was conducting spare-time warfare on theatre and cinema queues, also on crowds leaving the pubs at closing time. At the same time Staff Captain Albert Osborn and Staff Captain Gordon Simpson were undoubtedly Divinely directed to arrange a 'Charabanc Crusade' [1] (of which I was fortunate enough to be a member,) over a wider area of East Anglia, which brought Christ to a multitude of souls—106 in Norwich alone. Towns and villages were invaded by these crusaders morning, noon and night, with outstanding response.

I believe God's strategy with those events was aimed at far wider issues, for the annual invasion of the fishing ports by thousands of Scottish fish-workers happened when the revival was getting into its stride. Douglas Brown had prolonged his campaign, all places of worship being thronged with seeking souls, great numbers of Scots among them.

The fishing season ended, the Scots carried the revival fire north and North Scottish towns and villages were aflame, converts 'went everywhere preaching the Lord Jesus', thousands being saved. At Peterhead six hundred seekers were registered, and the Wick Salvation Army Corps saw at least five hundred, and great numbers of professing Christians were revived; practically all denominations pulsated with new life, and eager converts carried the gospel to their neighbouring villages.' [2]

After that first remarkable gathering in the Baptist Church, meetings continued there with overflowing crowds eager to hear the gospel. The Congregational Church was also brought into use as its minister, the Rev. Thomas Johnstone, joined with the Baptist Pastor in the work. Towards the end of November open air services were started in Saltoun Square, attended by hundreds of people, scores of them being saved by Christ. Now the Yarmouth converts were returning home to Fraserburgh and Jock Troup was joined by Willie Bruce, another preacher who had earlier assisted him at Yarmouth. Bruce was also a cooper and had formerly been a dancer and roller-skater.

By December the Baptist and Congregational Churches were both too small, and the final meetings were held in the Parish Church. An invitation had come from Dundee which Jock felt he should accept, so he and Willie Bruce now took leave of the people of Fraserburgh at an intensely moving farewell meeting. As their train drew out of the station, crowds on the platform were singing 'God be with you till we meet again'.

Wick

Far up on the north-east coast of Scotland stands the town of Wick where Jock Troup had worked as a cooper and where he had begun to preach the gospel in the Salvation Army Hall. After he and the other fisherfolk left for Yarmouth in 1921, a group of Welsh Pilgrim Preachers held meetings in the Baptist Church and in the open air, with the result that a number of young people had professed conversion. At the same time God was also moving down in Yarmouth where a number of men from Wick were wonderfully saved through the preaching of Douglas Brown. At one time the entire crew of the Wick motor drifter *Brae Flett*, owned by the Flett brothers, were converted men. When the fishermen returned north, the Pilgrim Preachers were still in the town. The Baptist Minister, the Rev. Millard, was often on the Salvation Army platform, and Captain Reid of the Salvation Army was equally at home in the Baptist pulpit at this time. So large were the crowds that meetings were held simultaneously in both places, as well as in the Rifle Hall. Remarkable scenes were witnessed on the last weekend of November with crowded meetings indoors and out, with tears of repentance and scores of converts. Cinemas and public houses lost their trade, and the lives of some of the most notorious characters in the community were transformed. At the traditional New Year's bonfire, instead of the customary drunken revelry, Salvation Army choruses were sung at an open-air rally.

Jock Troup returned to Wick early in January, after preaching in Dundee. It was not long before the strain began to tell on him and he developed throat trouble, which needed surgery and rest. When he was fit again he resumed his preaching with renewed vigour and held powerful meetings in the Rifle Hall each night, followed by open-air rallies lasting from nine till eleven. There are eye-witness reports of people falling down under conviction of sin and crying to God for mercy. When Jock left Wick in 1922 it was to embark upon his long preaching and evangelistic career, first in Scotland and later on both sides of the Atlantic.

Eyemouth

There were scenes of great rejoicing when the first boats returned to Eyemouth, north of Berwick-on-Tweed. As the vessels approached the quay the sound of singing could be heard coming over the water:

Love lifted me! Love lifted me!
When no one but Christ could help,
Love lifted me!'

Fathers and husbands who had been mightily moved by the Spirit of God at Yarmouth, were now completely transformed. Ten years later Jock Troup visited Eyemouth for a mission and the Spirit of Revival was still evident in the little fishing port. The local Methodist Minister, who told

Jock that he was one of the first to be saved at Yarmouth, was still firmly on the Christian pathway. In the Market Place at Eyemouth Jock stood on the seat of a Baby Austin, with his head and shoulders through the roof, to preach to the crowds. Dr. James Alexander Stewart, who was present on that occasion, reported: 'It was a typical fishing town of some two thousand population, though one could easily say that when Jock stood in the market square to preach, not less than three thousand gathered about him.' 3 The people already loved him for the blessing he had brought to their loved ones at Yarmouth in 1921 and now, ten years later, many more sinners found their way to the Saviour.

There were many other ports along the shores of the Firth of Forth to which men and women returned following their conversion in East Anglia; like Mussleburgh and Fisherow on the south side and Pitenween on the north. One shining example was John Hughes of Pitenween. His daughter came home from school one night in November 1921 to find her mother sitting in a chair crying—but they were tears of joy because she had received a letter from her husband to say he had been converted at Yarmouth the previous week-end.

At Winnyfold on the Aberdeenshire coast there had been people praying since the turn of the century for God to do a mighty work there. As usual a number of fisherfolk left in September 1921 to follow the shoals of herring south to Yarmouth. It was not long before news was returning that those prayers were being answered as so many of their people were being converted to faith in Christ.

Peterhead

Peterhead was one of the largest fishing ports on the north-east coast of Scotland. Many men, hardened and embittered by their experiences in the Great War, sailed south to Yarmouth for the 1921 herring season. So great was the power of God that while they were there whole crews were converted and their lives transformed. Sixty years later some still remained to give their first-hand testimony to the grace of God in those days. Among them was David Cordiner who was saved when he was a quiet lad of thirteen in the Baptist Church at Peterhead. He became a fisherman and attended the meetings at Yarmouth. While he was on board his drifter God spoke to him, and he had an inward conviction that God wanted him to become a preacher of the gospel. As they neared home he shared this vision with his shipmates, but they said he was too quiet a man for such work. However, he was not deterred. In fact he was more determined than ever to preach because he was haunted by a line of the old hymn:

'Must I go and empty-handed?
Must I meet my Saviour so?
Not one soul with which to greet Him;
Must I empty-handed go?"

When he arrived home he told his mother of God's dealings with him, but she too told him he would never make a speaker. In spite of these discouraging comments Davie Cordiner was to preach effectively to large crowds in Peterhead, mainly in the open air. 'Before I went to Yarmouth,' he confessed, 'I could not, and would not speak in the Salvation Army meetings. Satan had me in his grip. But God did a work in me at Yarmouth one night, and I re-dedicated my life to Christ and His service.' [4] David Cordiner was used by God in Peterhead just as Jock Troup was used by Him at Yarmouth and Fraserburgh. 'For six weeks meetings went on every night, David bearing the greater share of the work but others also coming to help, and hundreds professed faith in Christ.' [5] These events took place towards the close of 1921, after the return of the fishermen from Yarmouth, and David Cordiner attributed the success of his work to God's dealings with him while he was down there.

Hopeman and Burghead

These two fishing villages are situated snugly at the top of the Moray Firth. When the boats came home from Yarmouth and the women had returned by train, there were moving scenes on the quay at Hopeman—while the crews waited for the tide to let them come in, those on shore could hear the men on the drifters singing gospel hymns, many with a new found faith.

At Hopeman there were large meetings in the church hall and in the open air and there was a march of witness when gospel hymns were sung. There were many professions of faith, some going back to the time in Yarmouth but there were also new converts. A fisherman gave testimony to a four hour meeting in Yarmouth which he attended. He saw men and women weeping over their sins. "It was the best four hours I ever spent but best of all, the next night I was saved."

There was a similar movement at Burghead following the return of the fisherfolk from Yarmouth. "I believe God is working" said one fisherman. People were leaving their mending lofts and making for the meeting to hear young fishermen speak.

JW Keddie has given a thrilling account of what happened at the Free Church where the minister was the Rev James Henry who had exercised a faithful ministry there since 1906, but was saddened by the lack of people being saved.

At the October Communion of 1921 James Henry apparently felt oppressed by the dearth of new witnesses. The minister assisting at that Communion season was the Rev David Mackenzie, then of Nairn and subsequently Principal of the Free Church College, Edinburgh. Mackenzie records that when he and Mr Henry went to the Saturday prayer meeting "a form stepped forward in the dark passage-way between the manse and the vestry. It was a young man who wished to confess love to Christ on the coming Sabbath. He was received, the only one, but he was the first-fruits of what was to come."

In point of fact that young man subsequently went forward for the ministry. His name was Alexander Tolmie and he served successively in Kirkaldy and Lybster between 1937 and 1955. After the Communion service on the Sabbath, Mackenzie and Henry retired to the drawing room where they talked over the spiritual state of the district, read together and prayed together. "At the December Communion." Says Mackenzie, "prayers were abundantly answered."

When the fisherfolk returned from Yarmouth that November it was clear that many had been touched by the power of the gospel. The Kirk Session Minutes record that so many men and women had been converted and desired to profess their faith in Christ, an additional Communion Service should be held in December that year. When the minister and Session began to receive the new converts that December, the task was considerable.

Ninety came forward to confess Christ as Saviour for the first time. Mackenzie states that "those who were present at the preparatory services of the December Communion that year, can remember how Mr Henry wept tears of joy as he welcomed ninety new communicants."

JW Keddie gave this account when he reviewed *A Forgotten Revival* in *The Monthly Record of The Free Church of Scotland*, March 1993.

Gardenstown

Along the north facing coast of Banffshire lie the fishing towns of Cullen, Portknockie and Findochty, and the villages of Gardenstown, (known locally as Gamrie), and Rennan. From these ports whole families would make their way annually to Yarmouth and Lowestoft for the herring fishing, and their children would spend the season attending the local schools. In 1921 when the boats and trains had all departed, the Salvation Army Officer at Findochty accompanied by a mother and her 'young lassie' were walking together up the hill to the Army Hall for the Sunday evening service. Feeling a little disheartened because they were expecting only a few to attend they suddenly stopped, fell on their knees and prayed that God would do something. He did—at Yarmouth and Lowestoft—and soon the fishing communities along the Banffshire coast were receiving letters and telegrams telling of the conversion of their friends and loved ones.

Hugh Ferguson the Scot would go on board the boats when they arrived to welcome the men, so they were naturally drawn to his church where they came under the influence of his preaching, and that of Douglas Brown who was also frequently there. The result was that God answered the prayer of the Salvation Army officer and men and women went back home to their wind-swept villages in the north with salvation in their souls. Gospel work continued in Gardenstown after the boats returned, and meetings were held in a hall called *The Castle Grant*, with many conversions to Christ.

The following is an extract from a letter written by Mrs. Mary Wiseman of Gardenstown in 1983:

'...When we came home, a Mr. Esson started a series of meetings in a hall called The Castle Grant. Every night the hall was packed and souls were being saved, both young and old. It was an experience one could never forget, and it made a great impact on our village and the towns round our coast. There was an organ in nearly every home and you would hear the families singing together and praising God for his goodness. I think it was the following year my husband was baptised at Lowestoft by Mr. Ferguson.'

Another letter from Gardenstown, written at the same time by the wife of George West, (known as 'Golden' after the drifter he skippered) recalls:

'A lot of young folk from here were saved at that time, my husband and I among them. I think most of them have gone to be with their Lord; they were faithful to their end so they have gone to their reward. One of the best-loved hymns at that time was 'Sweeping through the gates of the New Jerusalem'.'

A postscript is added to this letter to the effect that George's brother, Joe West, (known as 'Deneside' after his drifter), had died on 30th April 1983 on his way to the Saturday prayer meeting. What an epitaph! Faithful in prayer for over sixty years!

Gardenstown became noted for the two strong evangelical congregations attending the Church of Scotland and the Brethren Assembly, and back in Lowestoft the effect of the revival among these Scottish fisherfolk was felt for years afterwards. Every Sunday evening in the herring season the Baptist Church was filled, usually by six o'clock, with chairs having to be placed down the aisles for the extra numbers, and until the service began at half past six the great building rang with hymn-singing reminiscent of the revival.

Inverallochy and Cairnbulg

In the late autumn of 1921, a Scottish newspaper carried a report of revival in Inverallochy and Cairnbulg, two rambling villages to the south of Fraserburgh:

'Since the boats returned, the devotions have risen to fever heat. The small Mission Hall has been crowded every night and four great outdoor meetings have been held each Sunday. Out of the 1,500 population, 600 conversions have taken place in a fortnight. Gambling has suddenly gone. Tobacco, pipes and cigarettes have been destroyed.'[6]

Pastor Fred Clarke, a Welshman, had conducted meetings in Cairnbulg in 1919, and had encouraged the converts to pray for revival. In the autumn of 1921 he returned with a Scotsman George Bell, to find that a reviving work of the Holy Spirit had begun in both villages. Then when the boats and crews returned from Yarmouth the powerful movement described in the press report took place.

Portsoy

Another fishing town on the north Banffshire coast where revival broke out as late as 1923 was Portsoy. There were many converts among their fishermen who went to Yarmouth and Lowestoft in 1921, and they returned home singing the songs of salvation, having left their old life of degradation and drink for the 'new life' in Christ. One of those Yarmouth converts was Jock Pirie who became the father-in-law of James Slater, the fisherman historian and poet, who was himself converted in the Portsoy revival. There the movement began in the spring of 1923 when the two Salvation Army Officers in charge of the Cullen Corps, Captain William Leed, affectionately known as 'The Giant', and his young assistant, Lieutenant Albert Townes, had the opportunity of preaching in Portsoy. Lieutenant Townes would pray into the night with tears for the souls of the people of Portsoy. After an introductory open-air meeting followed by an indoor gathering which attracted a great crowd, the young officer was given permission to conduct Sunday services in Portsoy. James Slater takes up the story:

'The open-air meeting commenced about 6 p.m. and followed the usual pattern; lively singing, simple testimonies by young converts from Cullen, a short message from Lieut. Townes, and an invitation to any present to accept God's offer of salvation. I can remember very little of what was said on that occasion: it had dawned on me that here was what I had been seeking and so far had failed to find. Just then there was a movement among the crowd and a young man went forward and knelt in the ring; a few minutes later he stood publicly to declare that he had accepted Christ as his Saviour. I could stand still no longer: I pushed my way into the ring, and as I knelt there I was shown the way of salvation by Lieut. Townes. I knew then I was 'saved by grace'. As I stood up, I heard the voice of the Lieutenant again, "Tell the folks that you have accepted the Lord Jesus as your Saviour." What a sea of faces confronted me as I gave my first stammering words of testimony.

This open-air meeting was a tremendous experience for the young officer as he saw all that he had hoped and prayed for brought to pass, especially so when we remember those who came to help him were young converts. How truly he here proved the truth of Scripture: "My strength is made perfect in weakness." (2 Corinthians 12:9) "Not by might, nor by power, but by My Spirit, saith the Lord of Hosts." (Zechariah 4:6)

I quote here from a letter I received from him in which he made reference to this occasion. He says, "Frankly I do not know how I coped with the situation, nor with the meeting later in the hall, but nothing is more certain than that there was another Presence guiding and directing."

From that open-air gathering the crowd flocked to the Christian Institute, to see again the evidence of the power of the Holy Spirit as six young folk were converted. This was the commencement of a spiritual awakening that continued for many weeks, during which time the hall was packed nightly and the open-air services drew great congregations. Many were converted at the time. Those who came from Cullen to conduct the meetings had to cycle daily in all weathers.' 7

There were many other villages, towns and cities in Scotland that were affected by revival in 1921-22. Places where the flame was lit from Yarmouth and Lowestoft have already been recorded here. Three ministers of the United Free Church visited the fishing towns on the Moray Firth and reported: 'To our minds, there is a genuine revival of religion, which is the work of the Spirit of God.' Numbers of inquirers were given in a report in *The Christian Herald*: there were 400 at Wick, 115 at Findochty, 242 at Peterhead and 79 at Cullen. 8

In December 1921, the city of Dundee was moved by the preaching of Jock Troup, Willie Bruce and David Cordiner. Every building they used was filled to overflowing. Meetings began with a period of spontaneous prayer, followed by hymn and chorus singing interspersed by the testimonies of recent converts. The preaching was the message of the Cross, after which streams of inquirers and converts made their way reverently, often with tears, down the aisles of the churches. Frequently the singing would start up again and services would continue into the night. The city was moved by the earnestness and sincerity of the fishermen preachers. One of the ministers said, 'It has been like Galilean days over again to have the young fishermen amongst us with the tang of the sea on their tongues, telling the old, old story with all the joy and enthusiasm of a new discovery.'

Early in 1922, the preachers moved on to Aberdeen, where they were joined by Douglas Brown. Similar scenes were witnessed and the revival continued there.

Glasgow, the largest city in Scotland, was reckoned to be the most evangelistic city in the world after the First World War. Churches and mission halls were crowded; large open air meetings were held; evangelists were preaching all over the city; converts were being added to the churches and built up in the faith. Jock Troup had already given an account of the work of God in the north-east to the General Assembly of the Church of Scotland, which met in the city. The warm-hearted cooper preacher was not overawed by the occasion, and some said he appeared before that august body wearing his fisherman's jersey!

Early in 1922, Jock Troup was invited to Glasgow by Peter McRostie, Superintendent of the Tent Hall, and Alexander Galbraith of the Seamen's Bethel. Meetings were held in the City Hall and the remarkable results that followed his preaching in East Anglia, north-east Scotland, Aberdeen and Dundee, were repeated. Although many ministers and churches put heart and soul into the work, some would not accept the young cooper preacher thundering out the gospel in such a centre of learning and culture as Glasgow.

Dr. James Alexander Stewart believed that, 'if the ordained ministers had left the work in the hands of the Holy Spirit', the revival would have spread through industrial Clydeside, on to the city of Edinburgh and all Scotland would have been shaken. In the event, the revival in the north-east and in the cities illustrated Paul's teaching in 1 Corinthians 1:27: 'But God hath chosen the foolish things of the world to confound the wise; and God hath chosen the weak things of the world to confound the things that are mighty.' Jock Troup declared, 'We are not revolting against the churches, but the Almighty is! The ministers have left the Bible for the new theology and are not preaching according to the Word as revealed. Not from the riches in the churches, but from among the lowly and humble, He has chosen His instruments to guide His people away from delusion to the

Light, back to the simple truth which is Christ.' 9

Both in the fishing ports, and in Glasgow when Jock became Superintendent of the Tent Hall, the atmosphere and effects of revival lingered for many years. This is convincing evidence that there was indeed a genuine revival in Scotland. If the Holy Spirit was poured out there in 1921-22, showers were still falling ten years later.

'This is the end'

W hat happened to the revival, and why did it not become nation-wide? If the movement in England did not develop into a national awakening, what was its full extent? In order to answer these questions we must trace God's dealings with Douglas Brown in England and Jock Troup in Scotland, for they were God's chief instruments in the revival in East Anglia throughout 1921. At the same time there was revival in Ulster where God raised up and used the Rev. William Nicholson with dramatic effect.

Douglas Brown in England

After the work of God in East Anglia in the spring and summer of 1921, Douglas Brown was in great demand for preaching missions all over the country. It was reported in *The Norfolk News and Weekly Press* on Saturday, September 10th, that he had received invitations from hundreds of places. Preaching missions were held in Southampton in October, followed by another in Bournemouth where congregations of three thousand attended the meetings and a large number of churches and ministers participated. According to the late Dr. J Edwin Orr, a leading writer on the subject of revival, Douglas Brown addressed gatherings as far afield as Aberdeen, Edinburgh, Liverpool, Newcastle and Birmingham, but the last weekend in February 1922 saw him back in Norwich, where he preached in St. Mary's Baptist Church to crowded congregations.

There were many indications that Douglas Brown was looking for revival throughout the land. In September 1921 he told *The Daily News* that whether the revival, which had already begun in East Anglia, spread nation-wide would depend to some extent on the message and the methods adopted by the churches. He warned against trying to organise revival instead of recognising that it was the work of God, and that His will and purpose determined its extent. He went on to lament the lack of power of the Holy Spirit in the churches, the modernistic teaching and the disunity among God's people. On several occasions Douglas Brown said that unless there was a revival in the land, he feared there would be revolution, due to the social unrest in the years following the Great War. Aware that he was in the midst of revival in East Anglia, he longed that it would sweep through the nation.

In 1922, Douglas Brown was invited to deliver a series of Bible Readings at the Keswick Convention. In May of that year, a letter of invitation to join in a day of prayer on the Saturday before it began, was sent by the Convention Council. This letter was included at the beginning of the official report *Keswick Week 1922*, and indicated the desire and hope on the part of very many Christians throughout the country for a nation-wide revival. The letter included this paragraph:

'Last year the account of the Revival in Lowestoft, given by two of our brethren, refreshed and encouraged many hearts; since then there have been further manifestations of God's saving power in the north-east of Scotland, and in Ulster, and also from many other parts of the land news has come of the moving of the Holy Spirit on the hearts of the people. At present there is a note of hope and expectation of coming blessing quite beyond anything that has been known amongst us for many years past. We thankfully acknowledge these signs of quickening, and yet we cannot shut our eyes to the terrible indifference and worldly-mindedness that are still prevailing so largely within the borders of the professing Church.'

The Convention that followed was the most remarkable in its forty-seven year history. It caused no surprise when Mr. Brown took 'Revival' as his subject, and it was said afterwards that there had been 'bombshells instead of Bible Readings'. A writer in *Keswick Week* wrote that the meeting for missionaries at seven o'clock on Friday morning was, for him, the most searching and revealing and uplifting of the gatherings of that week. With the tops of the mountains covered in clouds, about two hundred made their way through the early morning rain to the Pavilion. At the close they fell on their knees as they sang, 'When I Survey the Wondrous Cross', and re-dedicated their lives to God.

This early morning meeting was a sequel to the 'wonderful' events of the previous day, when 'the high-water mark was reached'. On that memorable morning, Douglas Brown had preached on 'Defective Consecration', based on the account of King Saul and the bleating sheep in 1 Samuel 15, telling

A Fraserburgh drifter entering Lowestoft harbour

how the King had failed to dedicate all the spoils of the conquest of the Amalekites to God. After a powerful appeal for utter surrender to God the preacher asked for a few moments of silent prayer. The report said there was such a stillness that the ticking of the clock sounded like a hammer beat.

'Stepping down from the platform, Mr. Brown invited all who were prepared to dedicate themselves wholly to the Lord, either for the first time or in a new way, to come forward and shake him by the hand and go straight to the Drill Hall.'

The Drill Hall, which was a short distance from the Convention tent, could accommodate no more than three hundred people. Before the preacher had ended his invitation the response began, and in a few moments 'the whole tent appeared to be in motion'. It would be impossible for all these people to get into the Drill Hall, so some were directed to the

Pavilion, while others remained in the tent. In all three places there was a great act of consecration by many hundreds of believers. The Convention had never before witnessed anything like this; some were bewildered, others were filled with holy joy, and a few felt that emotion had taken over. Clearly God had moved powerfully, and this event showed that there was a great longing for revival in many parts of the country.

In one of his addresses at Keswick in 1922, Mr. Brown said:

'I believe that in a very short time we are going to see the greatest spiritual awakening that has ever taken place in the history of our land....It may be when the veil is drawn asunder, when the church has been made ready, when the time has come for God to act and take the cataract off the eye of the nation....I care not how it comes; I care not what method is adopted so long as it is in accordance with the will of the Spirit of God. I feel the day is drawing swiftly near when men will sink their differences and come together to a place called Calvary, and there repent of their own foolishness of days gone by and, looking up into the face of God's anointed, shall say, "Thy kingdom come".' [1]

Douglas Brown's language seems extravagant now because there was no nation-wide revival. Nevertheless, the desire was there and he believed that God was able to do this great thing. Up to this time he had seen God working in reviving and saving power in Lowestoft, all round East Anglia and in north-east Scotland. He had also experienced something of the unity amongst Christians for which he longed, especially at Lowestoft, where ministers and congregations of different denominations were drawn together by the Gospel and the Cross of Christ. Why then were the hopes of Douglas Brown and so many Christians, for revival across the nation, not realised?

According to Montague Micklewright, who assisted Douglas Brown at Lowestoft, his preaching missions were taken over by a committee. It consisted mainly of Non-conformists but it was chaired by an Anglican, Dr. J Stuart Holden, Vicar of St. Paul's Portman Square. These men had a genuine concern for the preaching of the gospel throughout the land but, quite unintentionally, they took over Douglas Brown and he was no longer free to be led by the Holy Spirit. This is how Mr. Micklewright saw the situation:

'When the committee in question was formed, Dr. JW Thirtle, the editor of *The Christian* and highly esteemed on both sides of the Atlantic, said 'This is the end', meaning, as I understood it, that organisation had taken over, and that the committee thought that the mere presence of a dynamic personality like that of Douglas Brown ensured continued revival. It was a sad misapprehension on their part as Dr. Thirtle's prediction was entirely fulfilled.'

In another address at the 1922 Keswick Convention, Mr. Brown took as his text, 'It seemed good to the Holy Ghost and to us...' Acts 15:28. He began by saying that when he was looking through his father's Bible, he found these words written beside that text, 'The senior partnership of the Holy Ghost.' In the days of revival when he was so obviously God's instrument, he exemplified the text and theme of that address, but when the committee which was formed became the 'senior partner', the revival movement came to an end. Dr. Thirtle's verdict was sad but true.

However, we must not assume that if Douglas Brown had not been taken over by a committee, the revival would have continued and become nationwide. He was utterly dependent upon the anointing of the Holy Spirit upon his preaching, and God's people were equally dependent upon Him to pour out His Spirit in an even greater measure. That did not happen.

For several months after the revival at Lowestoft, Douglas Brown only occupied the pulpit of his church in Balham on the first Sunday of each month. At the Keswick Convention in 1922 he said that he had preached at seventeen hundred services since the beginning of 1921. The course of events after that Convention is not clear. He suffered a breakdown in health and was ordered to rest; he went to sea several times and took a holiday in the Canary Islands. As a young man he had been in the Merchant Service and he found that life at sea was beneficial to his health. In 1897, when he was only twenty three, Douglas Brown had had to resign from his first pastorate at Herne Bay because of ill-health. When he was Pastor of Kensington Baptist Church Bristol, where he attracted huge congregations, he again had to rest for a period. Montague Micklewright observed that throughout his ministry Douglas Brown had suffered from neuritis, which appeared to be due to an excess of nervous energy, but seemed to be relieved by much preaching.

In 1923, Mr. Brown became more deeply involved in organisation when he agreed to act as Commissioner for Evangelism for the Baptist Union. Accompanied by Dr. JC Carlisle he went to Canada in 1928, where he represented the Baptist Union at the opening ceremony of York Minster, Toronto. He conducted a mission lasting ten days, delivered a series of lectures at McMaster University and had the honorary degree of Doctor of Divinity conferred upon him. The Baptist Union honoured him with the presidency in 1929. During his remaining years at Balham Dr. Brown continued to be troubled by ill-health and in 1934, to his congregation's great regret, he moved to a less demanding ministry at Frinton-on-sea in Essex. His grand-daughter remembers him at Frinton as energetic enough to cycle about and to take an active part in the summer work of the Children's Special Service Mission. He also raised money for a clock tower which stands as a memorial to him, and enjoyed playing croquet. It does seem that the former flaming evangelist was mentally, emotionally, and to some extent spiritually, exhausted, and that God's time for him had come to an end. Frinton photographs show a man aged and drawn, in contrast to the handsome features of his earlier, more vigorous days. He passed to his reward on 27th April 1940, aged sixty six.

It seems a rather sad end for such an eminent servant of God. A retired Baptist minister, Rev. David Pearce, heard Dr. Brown preach on the Isle of Wight sometime between 1929 and 1933 and noticed a lack of spiritual power. He also heard of a ministers' meeting in which Douglas Brown said with tears, 'Pray for me, I have lost my power.' Was there some personal failure on the part of the preacher? Or had organisation and the denomination taken him over? On the other hand, as God is sovereign in revival, there can be a sudden ceasing of His power which is not necessarily due to any sin in His servant.

We must not lose sight of all that God did through Douglas Brown. He began his ministry at Herne Bay in 1895, from where he moved to Splott Road, Cardiff, in 1898. Called to Kensington, Bristol, the following year, his outstanding gifts as a preacher became very evident, and on Sunday evenings the church was packed half an hour before the service began. In those early days he went to sea with the White Star Line to recover his health. He did his greatest work at Balham where he ministered for twenty seven years, from 1907 to 1934. Within eighteen months of his arrival the seating capacity of the church had to be increased from five hundred to eight hundred, and for years a Sunday without conversions was rare. It was at Balham that God dealt with him, thrusting him out into mission work in East Anglia and pouring out His Spirit in revival power. It was following that revival that the church in Balham reached its peak membership of 1,005 in 1923.

A few personal reminiscences and anecdotes will show something of Douglas Brown's personality and character. He had a great love for the sea and installed a ship's wheel on the landing of his manse in London. Montague Micklewright described him as 'A very affectionate and loyal friend; full of sympathy for his fellow ministers and his congregation; winsome and sensitive; a handsome man.' He is also remembered by Gordon Wooderson, who was a young man in his church: 'Many times I have sat on the floor of the pulpit and watched the preacher's feet! I sat under him and gave thanks to the Lord for his faithful preaching, which was always from the Word. He would often raise his Bible aloft and say in his strong voice, "Man, if you tear this book to pieces, one day it will tear you to pieces."

When he was in Lowestoft, Douglas Brown stayed at the Royal Hotel where his very presence had a considerable effect. One of the staff, a chamber-maid, said to him one day, 'Mr. Brown, on a wall in the kitchen is a notice: 'Remember Room 59'. When any offensive remark is made, the speaker is pointed to that notice.' Room 59 was Douglas Brown's room! Relating this incident, he continued, 'Thank God I didn't play the fool.'

In the first quarter of this century Arthur Douglas Brown was undoubtedly one of the most powerful, compelling and widely-used preachers of the gospel in this country. His ministry is well summed up in the 1941 edition of the Baptist Union Hand-Book:

'It was there (at Balham) that he consumed himself by his zeal and passion for preaching, much of which he inherited from his father, the Rev. Archibald G Brown. He was firstly an evangelist sent 'to preach the Gospel, not with wisdom of words, lest the Cross of Christ should be made of none effect.' He was greatly used in the revival in East Anglia and many parts of our nation.'

Although the revival in which he was used never extended nation-wide, such an out-pouring of God's Spirit on a man's preaching in this country has not been seen since.

Jock Troup in Scotland

After an elementary education, an apprenticeship as a cooper and service with the Royal Navy in the First World War, Jock Troup was called from the fish-curing yards at Yarmouth to give himself wholly to preaching the gospel in a time of revival. In many ways like the fishermen of Galilee called from their nets by Jesus, these young fishermen led by Jock, participated in this historic period of gospel preaching in Scotland. They were entirely dependent upon the enabling power of the Holy Spirit and would happily have been identified with the apostles Peter and John as 'unlearned and ignorant men.' (Acts 4 :13) It was, however, felt by many that Jock Troup would benefit from a Bible College training, and after much prayer he entered the Glasgow Bible Training Institute in 1922. His testimony to the value of this time was that it laid the foundation for the whole of his future ministry. However, he proved a difficult student for the wise and godly principal, Dr. David McIntyre, to handle. He would have prayer meetings in his room late into the night and, as he prayed with the same fervour as he preached, it was difficult for those who were not in the prayer meetings to sleep! He would also be absent from classes for days and weeks at a time because he was preaching and evangelising.

In 1924 Jock left the Glasgow Bible Training Institute without a certificate, but with a very warm letter of commendation from Dr. McIntyre. While at the college, he had a powerful influence for good over his fellow students, and it was there that he met Peter Connolly (later Dr. Peter Connolly of the Baptist College, Springfield, Missouri, USA) who was to become his fellow-worker and life-long friend. God used them powerfully in and around Glasgow in 1922, 1923 and 1924.

Connolly commented on this period:

'We have spent nights in prayer together and together we have laboured in evangelism. We have known experiences when our faces were flushed with victory, moving in the flames of true revival, seeing men and women in hundreds under the converting influence of the Gospel. On the other hand, we have known periods of leanness of soul when the battle was tough and the situation called for an all-night of prayer. In the days of the Scottish Revival, I have seen my friend weep so long and uncontrollably that his eyes were like balls of fire as he went into the pulpit.' [2]

John Moore, a former Superintendent of the Tent Hall and many years Jock's junior, remembered his preaching:

'As a young convert, I used to make my way into Glasgow on Saturday afternoons just to hear Jock Troup in the open air at Glasgow Cross. What a treat it was! With his banjo he only had to sing a few lines of a well known hymn and the crowds gathered. His voice, strong, rich and resonant, soared above the busy traffic of the city and carried with it an appeal which never failed to reach the heart.[3] Through his ministry many souls were born again at this famous landmark.

Dr. James Stewart recalled the first time he heard Jock preach in Glasgow in 1927. He gave a graphic account of the experience:

'The building was packed with hundreds of people when I arrived so that it was only with difficulty that I managed to get a seat....I shall never forget the fervour and zest with which the fisherman-revivalist, with strength of purpose, left his seat and rushed to the pulpit, where he entered right into the heart of his message without preliminaries....

What a voice was his! It was the noisiest I had ever heard, and his words came tumbling out like machine-gun fire with their rich northern accent....After three-quarters of an hour of thundering forth the message with breathless speed, he suddenly paused. It was as if we had just passed through an earthquake, the silence in the great building was so keenly felt. Then, with tears rolling down his cheeks he pleaded with sinners to receive Christ as their Saviour right then and there.' [4]

Wherever Jock went, the Holy Spirit seemed to move powerfully. Eventually, in 1932 he was invited to assist at the Tent Hall under Peter McRostie, who died the following year. Jock then took over the full responsibility and continued there until 1945. After retiring from the Superintendency of the Tent Hall he undertook an itinerant ministry on both sides of the Atlantic. The Rev. Tom Paterson, who lived near Jock in Glasgow, has told how he specially loved to get back among the fisherfolk upon whom he had first seen God pour out His Spirit. Although the revival was widespread in Scotland, it was among those fishing communities along the north-east coast that the influence of the reviving Spirit of God seemed to last the longest. Tom Paterson also described Jock as reticent in speaking about the revival in later years, as though it was too sacred and awesome to talk about. On 18th April 1954, he was preaching at the Knox Presbyterian Church, Spokane, Washington, on 'Ye must be born again', when he suddenly came to the end of his earthly course.

Peter Connolly gave this epitaph for his friend:

'He was a preacher—a Gospel preacher—a rugged Gospel preacher. That very ruggedness revealed a rustic beauty in the Gospel message he preached....Jock Troup, from the hour of his conversion, had a divine tongue put in his mouth, and nothing but death could silence him.' 5

The Rev. WP Nicholson, Northern Ireland

There was another revival movement that must be mentioned in order to give a full picture of the powerful workings of God's Holy Spirit in the British Isles in 1921. This was in Ulster under the Rev. WP Nicholson, who was to that Province what Douglas Brown was to England and Jock Troup was to Scotland. William Patteson Nicholson was born in Bangor in 1876; his father was a sea captain and his mother was a most godly woman who prayed for her son's conversion. William himself went to sea and took to drink, but when he was twenty three years old 'he was converted' at home in Bangor. Two years later, in 1901, he entered the Glasgow Bible Training Institute, after which he did evangelistic work in Lanarkshire, and then in Melbourne, Australia. Nicholson went to the United States where he was ordained a Presbyterian Minister in Carl, Pennsylvania, in 1914, and then served on the staff of the Bible Institute of Los Angeles.

Parliamentary autonomy was granted to Northern Ireland in 1921, but the IRA did its utmost to make the Province ungovernable. There was fighting in the streets with bombing and sniping by gunmen at police and at passers-by. Protestants were being murdered in Catholic counties, and they in turn were ill-treating innocent Catholic families. The land was full of bitterness, hatred and sectarian violence.

It was at such a time, and in answer to the fervent prayers of God's people, that William Nicholson began to preach the gospel in Ulster with great power and effect. Many believed that what happened was nothing short of a Heaven-sent revival which was instrumental in saving the Province from far greater blood-shed and destruction. WP Nicholson returned from America and began evangelistic work, first at Bangor in 1920 and then in Portadown in May 1921, where there were crowded congregations and scores of conversions. It is significant that this was just two months after God had poured out His Spirit on the east coast of England.

Missions were held at Lurgan, Lisburn and Newtownards; wherever William Nicholson preached hundreds were converted and whole communities were affected. In 1922, when unrest and violence were at their height, and with murder and destruction of property going on all around, WP(as he was known) preached in Belfast. Meetings were held in the Albert Hall on the Shankill Road, which was notorious for trouble. Each night up to three thousand people filled that great auditorium, and during that series of meetings more than two thousand passed through the inquiry rooms. In East Belfast, where men marched to the services in their working clothes, there was such a crush of shipyard workers who wanted to hear the gospel that the gates of the church were pushed over and the pillars moved. Enormous crowds were also drawn to Londonderry, Ulster's second city, and to Ballymena and Carrickfergus.

William Nicholson was a colourful character. His language was sometimes crude and vulgar, and he could be very offensive. At times he would be extremely jocular, and then without warning the atmosphere would change as he warned of judgement and appealed to people to come to Christ. An example of his method was the way in which he dealt with a wife whose husband beat her. 'Bring him to the meeting and give me a nod,' he told her. The nod was duly given one evening, and although the man's name was not mentioned, he was given a dressing down from the pulpit. WP went on to say that he would watch the man and if he put ten shillings in the offering plate he would not be named! That night the offering plates were full of ten shilling notes!

The impact of Nicholson's preaching on the lives of the people was seen in the reports of business men who, having written off bad debts, received their money from creditors whose consciences had been awakened. The story was also told of the publican who was saved and then poured his liquor down the drain and closed his public house.

There was no doubt in the mind of Dr. J Edwin Orr that revival occurred in Ulster from 1921 to 1923. He himself was converted at the time, though not in one of WP Nicholson's campaigns. He wrote:

'Nicholson's missions were the evangelistic focus of the movement; 12,409 people were counselled in the inquiry rooms; many churches gained additions, some a hundred, some double; twenty new societies of Christian Endeavour were started; prayer meetings, Bible classes and missionary meetings all increased in strength; Presbytery's first communicant figures were 4,741 added in 1920, 4,935 more in 1921. 6,360 in 1922 and 6,059 in 1923. Ministerial candidates doubled.' [6]

After 1921 the tide of spiritual blessing seemed to ebb somewhat, although WP Nicholson continued to preach the gospel with considerable success. He was a frequent visitor to Scotland, where Jock Troup invited him to preach in the Tent Hall. Thus the over-all picture of revival in the United Kingdom is completed and it is now clear that in three areas, and through three men in particular, God moved in power, beginning in Lowestoft in the first week of March 1921.

The fruits of Revival

Lowestoft

A t Lowestoft, the long term results of the revival were not spectacular, but the spiritual life of the churches which were involved received a boost which was evident for years. Thirty-eight added to the membership of the Baptist Church in 1921 seems a small number, but there were many more new converts scattered throughout the participating churches, both in the town and further afield. The Lowestoft Baptist church had a widespread reputation for the strength of its prayer meeting, its Biblical preaching and its evangelistic zeal. Open-air preaching was a feature of the life of the church, and a large number of lay-preachers regularly went out to the mission halls and country chapels around the area. The huge Sunday School had no fewer than six hundred children on the registers, and an average attendance of four hundred and fifty. In 1934, after seventeen years, Hugh Ferguson's ministry closed with three hundred on the church roll, compared with two hundred when he started. He was followed by Rev. W Thorrington Cork, who baptised fifty-five people in the first two years of his ministry.

Another feature of the post revival period was the stream of men and women from Lowestoft who were called to serve God at home and abroad. Frank Chaplin was baptised by Hugh Ferguson and, after Bible College training, joined The Bolivian Indian Mission. The Rector of Oulton, Rev. Henry Martin, conducted a stirring valedictory service. Converted in that first memorable week, Robert Browne became a Wycliffe Preacher before entering the ministry of the Baptist Church. He also became a hymn writer. George Sterry, Superintendent of the enormous Baptist Sunday School, offered himself for missionary service but, being physically unfit, he entered the home ministry. Two other men who entered the ministry were Arthur J Barnard and, later, WL Wagnell.

In 1923, Rev. John Hayes, Vicar of Christ Church and a close friend of Ferguson, left Lowestoft. He was followed by a succession of staunch evangelical vicars. This church, the most easterly in the British Isles, also sent a number of men and women into the ministry and to the mission field. One of

Putting to sea 1921

them was Canon Alan Neech, a Lowestoft boy who became Bishop of Benares, India; he later became General Secretary of The Bible Churchman's Missionary Society and was Chairman of The Keswick Convention Council. Another was Ralph Miles who was called to serve God in China, but was invalided home after two years and died while a curate in Edgeware. Dorothy Leader, also from Christ Church, went to India, followed by James Garrood and Molly 3 Holder. These two married but when they had to return to England because of Mr Garrood's health, they worked together in a country parish. John Bishop was another local boy who was called to the ministry, to spend a life-time serving God in this country.

In the village of Oulton, on the outskirts of Lowestoft, Rev. Henry Martin maintained a fervent and effective ministry until he died of cancer in 1929. Rose Sturman, who was converted in Mrs. Martin's Bible Class and attended the revival meetings with her, became a BCMS missionary teacher in a school for the deaf in Rangoon. Another young convert from the revival was Percy Smith, who became the highly respected Captain of the Oulton Boys' Brigade Company until, well into middle life, he was ordained into the ministry.

After the departure of Rev. WG Hardie from St. John's Church, where the largest revival meetings had been held, that church's long evangelical tradition seemed to wane. There were however, other churches, like the Primitive Methodists and the assemblies and missions, which maintained a strong gospel witness in the town and district. Every autumn through two decades until the Second World War, the Scottish fisherfolk brought a breath of revival with them when they arrived for the 'home fishing'. They thronged the churches and assembly halls, particularly the Baptist Church, and their singing was unforgettable. Even after the war the churches which featured in the revival were still together, and for years a monthly meeting, known as Saturday Rendez-vous, filled the Baptist Church and earned a country-wide reputation.

Another remarkable echo of revival days occured in 1946. During the war, the cinemas in Lowestoft were opened on Sundays for the entertainment of the thousands of service men and women who were based in the town, which was the Headquarters of the Royal Naval Patrol Service. After the war, a referendum was held to decide whether the cinemas should remain open on Sundays, or revert to the pre-war practice and close. The churches that had come together in 1921 were together again twenty five years later, and the ministers put up a staunch defence of the Lord's day, although they lost the battle. They were the late Frank Kinsbury, Baptist; the late Stanley Pert, Oulton, and Harry Sutton, Vicar of Christ Church. On one occasion Frank Kinsbury preached on the pavement outside the Marina cinema and was heckled by the manager. On the Saturday before the vote, he doughtily set up a loud-speaker in the doorway of the Baptist Church and broadcast up and down the main street, 'Use God's day in God's way; vote against Sunday cinemas!'

Ipswich

One of the most outstanding evangelists in this country between the wars was Rev. Lionel B Fletcher, a Congregational Minister who was born in

Australia. He brought his family to Britain in 1916 at the urgent request of Wood Street Congregational Church Cardiff, and began to conduct missions in England in 1921. One of the first was in Ipswich in the autumn, just four months after the revival. An open-air service on the Cornhill was attended by thousands. Lionel Fletcher's preaching meetings were held at Tackett Street Congregational Church, where the Friday evening service was particularly notable, with the building packed both upstairs and down. At the close, a group of local sportsmen responded to the preacher's invitation and marched down the aisle to shake his hand. They were led by Rowland (Bert) Haste, Ipswich Town footballer and leading goal scorer. Here is his own testimony:

'I was greatly blessed by having godly parents, and my dear mother invited me to attend the campaign. Each night I accompanied her. Throughout each meeting a battle raged in my heart. On Friday, September 30th, 1921, at 8.40 p.m., while the audience sang the closing hymn, 'Yet there is room', my thoughts carried me back to the Flanders' mud, to that gun pit where I had made a definite promise which had never been fulfilled. There and then I walked forward to the platform, prompted by the Holy Spirit, and gripped the Missioner's hand as an indication that 'the great transaction' was done, and that I was the Lord's.....As my dear mother and I journeyed home arm in arm from that church where I had been set at liberty, I felt that I must tell the stones in the street the story of my deliverance.'

In 1928, Bert Haste went to India with the Bible Churchman's Missionary Society.

From 1921 to 1923 Lionel Fletcher conducted missions throughout Britain before returning to Ipswich and preaching in nearby towns. At Stowmarket, in January 1923, the church was closed an hour and a half before the service was due to begin. The proprietor of a picture house cancelled a showing and offered the use of his building. So many people wanted to attend that tickets were issued for a second session, and as the first congregation left, another entered. In December 1923, the Minister of the Congregational Church sent a letter of encouragement to one hundred young people who had been converted during the mission of the previous January.

In his book, *Mighty Moments*, Lionel Fletcher recorded a remarkable movement of the Holy Spirit in a town near Ipswich. On the last night of what had been a difficult mission the leaders were expecting a break-through as there had been a fervent spirit of prayer. However, when Mr. Fletcher closed the service nothing happened, and, although the meeting was over, the members of the congregation remained firmly in their seats. Thinking there were some who wished to yield to Christ, the Evangelist gave out a hymn and made a further appeal, but still there was no response. After repeating the process with the same result, he left the building, followed a few minutes later by the congregation. Mystified by these events, Mr. Fletcher and local leaders decided to give themselves to prayer. He was awakened early the following morning with the news that a village minister had been roused during the night by a group of young men who wanted him to pray with them. It then became apparent that in a number of places, ministers were being called upon by people who needed spiritual help. This continued in the weeks that followed as blessing swept the district.

Lionel Fletcher did not see his work in East Anglia as revival, but rather its aftermath. He said that Douglas Brown had been used 'most wonderfully' on the east coast, and that people were asking, 'Will this revival sweep Britain?' Asked about the work of Fletcher in East Anglia, M J Micklewright commented, 'The movement in which he participated was quite different from that in Lowestoft. One can only emphasise the unique character of the movement in which Douglas Brown was involved, which was dependent solely upon preaching inspired by the Holy Spirit, until the revival ceased.' Lionel Fletcher's evangelistic preaching developed until, in the 1930s, he became British Empire Evangelist with The Movement for World Evangelisation.

Nation-wide evangelism

Although the revival of 1921 did not sweep the nation, there was a tide of evangelism that continued through two decades until the beginning of the Second World War.

An interdenominational youth movement known as The National Young Life Campaign, founded by Arthur and Frederick Wood, received a great impetus after the revival of 1921. An All Round London Campaign was arranged as revival broke out on the east coast. It was followed by campaigns in many towns and cities, including Liverpool where four hundred churches participated. Great meetings were held in the Philharmonic Hall, where there were thirteen hundred professions of faith. In the 1920s, the Wood brothers also conducted meetings in Lowestoft and, even more, in Norwich, where an outstanding campaign was held in St. Andrew's Hall in the centre of the city. It had warm support from Canon Hay Aitken of Norwich Cathedral, who had been involved in the revival. There were crowded audiences and many conversions. Bible study circles were organised in Colman's Mustard Factory and in Caley's Chocolate Factory, and new NYLC branches and church groups were formed with five hundred members. Striving to reach the youth of the country for Christ, Frederick Wood was greatly encouraged by the revival ministry of Douglas Brown, whom he quoted in *Youth Advancing*, the story of the movement. 'Any denomination which could remain unmoved and complacent when its young life was drifting away by thousands, and which refused to face the ugly facts, was suffering from sleeping sickness. Organised religion needs a Pentecost.'

Another evangelist who rose to prominence in 1923 was the daughter of William Booth, Mrs. Catherine Booth-Clibborn, known as 'La Marechale'; she was the founder of the Salvation Army in France and Switzerland. Through the twenties she campaigned in many large towns in England, as well as in Aberdeen, and in Belfast—where she combined with WP Nicholson and made an impact on the city at a troubled and violent time.

Gipsy Rodney Smith, a genuine Romany, must rank highly in power and effectiveness as an evangelist in this country and other parts of the world. He began his ministry in the Salvation Army in the nineteenth century, and ended it in Methodism in the twentieth. When revival broke out in 1921, Gipsy Smith was sixty and he supported Douglas Brown in his home town of Cambridge. It is interesting that a biographer refers to the 1920s as Gipsy Smith's 'golden years', [1] in which he preached with renewed vigour, urging sinners to repent and believers to seek holiness of life. He held missions in London, in the Kingsway Hall in 1923, and in the Albert Hall in 1924. Thousands of his hearers professed faith, and many more believers re-dedicated their lives to Christ. In 1935 Gipsy Smith held a mission in

Lowestoft and Oulton during the herring season when the Scottish fishermen were in the town. The meetings were crowded, and there are converts alive today who still have vivid memories of his preaching and singing.

The outstanding evangelical layman in England of the twentieth century has been A Lindsay Glegg. An aristocrat and industrialist, he was converted at the Keswick Convention during the Welsh Revival in 1905. As well as superintending the Down Lodge Hall Mission in Wandsworth, a working-class district of London, he preached two hundred and fifty times a year for thirty years. As President of British Christian Endeavour, Lindsay Glegg directed an evangelistic drive for the nation's youth in 1931, and the preachers included F P Wood, Lionel Fletcher, Gipsy Smith and WY Fullerton. The meetings drew large crowds, and there were hundreds of inquirers and professions of faith.

While Lindsay Glegg was little known outside this country, there were other British evangelists who were used worldwide, among whom were J Sidlow Baxter, JD Blinco, Bryan Green, Roy Hession, J Edwin Orr, Alan Redpath, Tom Rees, James Stewart and Ian Thomas, all of them active for a generation...Some had been converted in the early 1920s.

In the early thirties, an evangelistic team of young Baptist pastors was formed. It was known as 'The Essex Five'. Following the first World War one of the members, Stanley Baxter, had received a remarkable call from God. As a young Christian and ex-service-man, shell-shocked and broken in spirit, he was taken to one of a series of special meetings in Bloomsbury Baptist Church in the centre of London. He sat in the gallery when suddenly the preacher, Douglas Brown, pointed a 'bony finger' at him and said, 'Young man, God wants you for a bit of movement!' The other members of the team were, Hugh McCullough, an ex-Royal Flying Corps pilot, George Banks, Tom Shepherd and Fred Missen. These men were released by their churches for a week in each month and the churches held a week of prayer while they were away. From 1933 to 1936 missions were held all over Essex and one in Wales. People flocked to the churches where the men were preaching and a considerable number of people were saved.

There were two outstanding Methodists in the two decades between the wars who, like the preachers in the revival, stood firm against the rising tide of liberal theology. Dr. Dinsdale Young was the Minister of Westminster Central Hall, London. One of the great preachers of his day, he was conservative in his theology with a great love for the Bible and for the Gospel, which, he said, was the only message he had to proclaim. His contemporary was Rev. Samuel Chadwick, who was not only a powerful evangelist himself, but also, as Principal of Cliff College, sent many more evangelists out into the country.

It was in London in 1925-26, that the young clinical assistant to Lord Horder, Dr. D Martyn Lloyd-Jones, was called to the Christian ministry. After twelve years in Wales, where he saw many souls saved during his ministry at Aberavon, he returned to London in 1938. He shared the ministry at Westminster Chapel with Dr. G Campbell Morgan until 1943, when he succeeded him as Pastor. Dr. Lloyd-Jones believed that the preaching of the Gospel was the primary Divine method of saving souls, and he had a continuing burden for revival. He therefore had much in common with the preachers of the revival of 1921, even though he differed from them in not making public appeals for an immediate, open response to the invitation of the Gospel.

In addition to the NYLC, other evangelistic societies flourished in England after the revival of 1921. They included The Evangelisation Society whose evangelists travelled all over Britain; The Movement for World Evangelisation, and the Children's Special Service Mission which was founded after the 1859 Revival and specialised in camps and beach missions. One of the most important evangelical movements started in Britain during the 1920s was the Inter-Varsity Fellowship, which was formed in 1928. In 1919 there had been a conference at Oxford organised by undergraduates of Oxford and Cambridge who wanted to see Christian Unions in all universities. The General Secretary of the influential but liberal Student Christian Movement claimed in 1920, 'The verbal inspiration of the Bible is as dead as Queen Anne.' The revivals at this time seem to have been a direct Divine answer to the liberal theology of the day. Under two medical graduates, Douglas Johnson and Howard Guinness, the IVF campaigned vigorously for evangelical truth. Dr. Howard Guinness was from the famous family of Gattan Guinness who had been a leader in the 1859 revival. Howard did a great evangelistic work among students at home and overseas. Another outstanding student evangelist in the late 1920s was Bryan Green. After five years in a South London parish, he organised student missions all over the country. A powerful thinker and an able speaker, he conducted many outstanding university missions. Sadly, he moved to the left in his theology and became known as a liberal evangelical.

Scotland

An Arts student from Glasgow University, DP Thomson—'a youthful giant'—was called by God to Fraserburgh in the days of revival in 1921. He was again involved in revival ministry in Aberdeenshire. After entering the ministry of the Church of Scotland at Dunfermline, he built an evangelistic base at Crieff in Perthshire, and was recognised as the Evangelist of the Church of Scotland. He was scholarly compared with the rugged Jock Troup, but together they were household names in Scottish evangelism through the 20s and 30s.

In the twenties the Rev. Tom Macbeath Paterson was an evangelist who preached in the fishing villages along the north east coast of Scotland. Souls were saved continually and pastors would frequently be knocked up in the night by people in distress about the state of their souls. He conducted a mission in Kilsyth in central Scotland during the same period, but there were few apparent conversions. When he returned years later, the pastor, Bill Kennedy, a converted soccer player, invited those who had been converted as a result of the earlier visit to stand. Tom Paterson was surprised to see a crowd of people rise to their feet.

No evangelistic society received more help and encouragement from the revival of 1921 than the Faith Mission, which was based in Scotland. At the close of that year, JG Govan, the founder, declared, 'It has been a good year, a very good year. This thirty-fifth year has surpassed any year in the last twenty or more of the Mission's history.' [2] In an article in the magazine *Bright Words,* the question was asked, 'Are we on the eve of revival?' Although there was no widespread national revival, the Faith Mission enjoyed a special time of Divine blessing. Its simple evangelistic methods of prayer and preaching were in line with the revival preachers, and it prospered in Scotland and Ulster. In East Anglia, pilgrims of the Mission in Suffolk said there were indications of a widespread movement of God. Work continued to grow until in 1925 an English District of the Faith Mission was formed. At Elmsett in Suffolk, two pilgrims of the Mission saw thirty-six come to Christ, and the place was revolutionised.

Although this survey is not comprehensive, it is wide ranging, and demonstrates that the revivals of 1921 were followed by a remarkable period of evangelistic activity in England, Scotland and Northern Ireland. It touched the great cities, the towns and the villages. Our largest auditoriums, churches, chapels and mission-halls were filled with people eager to hear the Gospel. Students in our universities, farm-workers and fisherfolk all heard the message. Dr. J Edwin Orr wrote:

'The revival awakenings of the early 1920s were soon forgotten by the people of God, who invariably forget the works of God; but they served His purpose in those times. Evangelism is an absolute necessity and a bounden duty, but it must be considered in terms of a revival awakening.' [3]

The last revival in England

In the history of revivals in Britain during the twentieth century, the 1921 Revival, which began in East Anglia, lies between the 1904 Revival in Wales and that of 1949 in the Scottish Hebrides. In the former the Holy Spirit came upon Evan Roberts, a probationary Calvinistic Methodist Minister, in a dramatic and powerful way in a crowded meeting. Prior to that experience he had been caught up in times of ecstatic communion with God in the night. 'Bend the Church and save the world' became the watchword of his revival ministry. The Holy Spirit took control of the meetings, where there was much more singing and praying than preaching, and more emphasis on experience than on faith and doctrine. Dr. Eifion Evans has said of the movement: 'While the revivalist's ideas were Biblical, they were cast in an experimental mould, a mould determined by Roberts' own spiritual pilgrimage and designed for the express purpose of reviving the Church.' [4] Scores of thousands professed faith and were added to the churches in Wales, especially the Calvinistic Methodists, and the social impact of the revival included an astonishing decrease in convictions for drunkenness. In some areas there was a shortage of biblical preaching and teaching, and this resulted in a spiritual decline in the churches. However it was clearly the most powerful work of the Spirit of God in Britain in the twentieth century up to that point.

The revival in the Scottish Hebrides in 1949 appears to have been the most Biblical and deeply spiritual movement of the three. It was prepared for by earnest prayer and born of a deep concern for the low state of God's people in the islands. For all its sound doctrine there was a deadness in the United Free Church, accompanied by a careless attitude towards Sabbath observance and public worship, and a consuming interest in worldly pleasure. When the revival came it was marked by an awesome sense of God's presence, followed by a deep spirit of repentance. There were physical manifestations of distress brought about by conviction of sin, and then of ecstasy as people entered into the joy and relief of knowing God's forgiveness. The Rev. Duncan Campbell, a former Free Church minister, came across from the mainland and preached with convicting, reviving and converting power, and parish ministers were revived with their congregations. In some places the community was deeply affected. An example was when a minister went into a dance hall after three o'clock in the morning, persuaded the dancers to sing a psalm, and gave a few words of exhortation. Suddenly the young men and women forgot their revelry and began to cry to God for mercy. This was a genuine revival, a spiritual awakening, a visitation from on high.

Although the movement in East Anglia may not have been as widespread as that in Wales, nor as intense as that in the Hebrides, it was nevertheless just as genuine. All such works of God are subject to criticism, not only from the unbelieving world but from the churches as well, and the East Anglian Revival was no exception. In an article entitled 'The Modern Revival of Religion', Dr. JC Carlile, President of the Baptist Union in 1921, dismissed the work in East Anglia as an 'emotional wave' produced by a 'hypnotic preacher'. In the same article he described Douglas Brown as his 'beloved friend'! The Lowestoft ministers were saddened and a joint letter appeared expressing their disappointment at what they considered to be a perversion of the truth. They wrote:

'The results are of the most tangible and convincing kind, and must carry conviction to the most sceptical observer. Christian ministers, and workers from other towns who

Lowestoft fishing industry 1921

have come to witness for themselves what has been taking place in this district, have not hesitated to declare, "This is the Lord's doing; it is marvellous in our eyes!".' 5

In a published statement, the Rev. John Hayes, Vicar of Christ Church, attempted to answer Dr. Carlile's criticisms. 'I almost despair of organised religion ... we need the church to be converted,' complained Dr. Carlile. 'This is just what we have been experiencing here in Lowestoft and district,' replied Mr. Hayes. 'People IN the churches have been converted.' In response to Dr. Carlile's appeal for the renewal of Apostolic preaching, John Hayes said that the message of the Apostles had been preached, including the Second Advent and its significance for Christians. For three weeks, including the Bank Holiday, Christ Church was filled every afternoon at three o'clock: 'We shall not soon forget the sound of hundreds of people turning the pages of their Bibles as they followed the preacher—

'to see if these things were so'. John Hayes concluded, 'No arrangements had been made for such an outpouring of the Holy Spirit's power. We just did our best to meet the situation and keep in the will of God. Many there were indeed, who came to scoff and to question, but they stayed to pray.' [6]

All revivals have their weaknesses because the people of God are sinners, saved by grace but not yet perfect. It is only by God's sovereign power that revivals happen, and they continue as long as He pours out His Spirit upon His people, which is usually for short periods. Dr. Carlile's assessment of Douglas Brown as a 'hypnotic preacher' was insensitive and prejudiced. There is no doubt that there were many people who were attracted by his striking appearance, winsome personality and eloquence, rather than by the Gospel he preached. At the same time, hundreds saw beyond the preacher to the Saviour to whom he pointed, and were drawn to Him as to a magnet. The preaching appealed strongly to the emotions; it was experiential and sprinkled with anecdotes. Neither the East Anglians nor the Scots are known for displaying their emotions, but there was plenty of quiet weeping in both communities when God was at work. There was no organised follow-up of converts in Douglas Brown's meetings as there is in modern evangelistic campaigns. Inquirers were counselled by ministers, experienced Christians, and by the preachers themselves; sometimes they had to be dealt with in groups because there were so many. This would be viewed as a serious weakness in the light of the elaborate follow-up methods employed in modern evangelism. However, John Wesley once said that the Holy Spirit followed up the converts from his preaching! There were weaknesses in the revival of 1921, and in the frail instruments which God chose to use. Sadly it was confined to certain local areas and did not spread throughout the country as praying people had hoped. Nevertheless, it was a revival in the Biblical sense, as the final chapter will try to demonstrate.

A Biblical perspective

In the opening verses of Psalm 85, God's people are exhorted to remember His past mercies.

LORD, thou hast been favourable unto thy land: thou
hast brought back the captivity of Jacob.
Thou hast forgiven the iniquity of thy people, thou
hast covered all their sin. Selah.
Thou hast taken away all thy wrath: thou hast turned
thyself from the fierceness of thine anger. (vv 1-3).

God had brought Israel out of captivity in Egypt and He had forgiven them again and again. Christians should constantly remember God's mercies in redemption and the forgiveness of sins through the death and resurrection of the Lord Jesus Christ. The psalmist was also aware that his people had sadly declined from what they once were and prayed, 'Wilt thou not revive us again....?' (v. 6). It is therefore important that when we pray for revival in our day, we remember past mercies in revival so that our reflection stimulates prayer, even though it is seventy years since we saw such a movement in England.

Where God had worked before

God often works in revival in the same place more than once. This is something that has happened throughout revival history, not least in East Anglia, and in Lowestoft in particular. What is known as the Second Evangelical Awakening began to sweep America and Britain in 1859 and reached East Anglia in 1861. In early February that year, two itinerant evangelists, Reginald Radcliffe and Shuldam Henry, visited Lowestoft for several days; the Town Hall was filled to overflowing, and by the following Sunday over one hundred inquirers had come to the notice of the ministers. Meetings continued daily after the evangelists moved on, and when they returned to the town, meetings were held in the Continental Goods Depot of the Eastern Counties Railway, where they were presided over by the Vicar of Lowestoft, the Rev. Francis Cunningham. Hundreds were anxious about their souls; a meeting at the Town Hall the following morning overflowed with inquirers and many fishermen were among the converts. It was reported in May that Lowestoft 'had been blessed beyond measure' with five hundred being added to the churches in the town, 'both established and dissenting'. [1]

Among the ten thousand inhabitants of Lowestoft, drunkenness declined, the police had fewer people to deal with from the dens of vice in the town and former blasphemers became men of prayer. Another itinerant evangelist, William Carter, preached to two thousand in the Railway Goods Shed and 'many were broken up and brought to Christ'. [2] On another occasion four thousand gathered, and it was said to have been one of the most solemn times ever experienced by Christians in the area. William Carter found many converts from Reginald Radcliffe's ministry and he said he had not been to any place where the testimony had been owned by God more than it had been in Lowestoft. It is interesting to note that two local churches which were prominent in the revival in 1921 were founded at this time. Christ Church was built in 1868 for the converts among the fisher-folk, the stone being laid in memory of Francis Cunningham who had drawn up the plans in 1864 when the revival was still in progress. The first Fishermen's Bethel was built in 1862 in Commercial Road, but it was a later congregation meeting in the present Bethel opposite the Fish Market that witnessed revival scenes in 1921. How much the 1860 revival affected the Baptist Church is unclear, except that CH Spurgeon, the great Baptist preacher, filled the Continental Goods Shed at the time, and the Baptist Church was cleared of debt as a result of his visit!

When the Rev. George Knight came from Mr. Spurgeon's Pastors' College in 1870 to take up the pastorate of the Baptist Church in Lowestoft, doctrinal confusion had brought decline and the membership had fallen to about forty. The new pastor gathered six or eight men around him to call upon God for help. It was during the Week of Prayer in January 1871, after George Knight had been preaching, that an officer from the Wesleyan Church walked forward to the communion rail, and so God began to move again in Lowestoft. This heralded a powerful work of the Holy Spirit in the Baptist Church, in which backsliders were restored, souls were saved and congregations overflowed. During the herring fishing season, when the

Scottish fishermen were in town, two services had to be held simultaneously on Sunday evenings, one in the church and the other in the Public Hall opposite. George Knight would preach in the Public Hall while a visiting preacher occupied the pulpit of the church. It is remarkable that another of Spurgeon's students, the Rev. Archibald J Brown of the East London Tabernacle, preached at the Baptist Church on special occasions and brought his family to the nearby village of Kessingland for holidays. His son, Arthur Douglas, was to be God's instrument for the revival fifty years later.

As the Christians in Lowestoft prayed for revival before its outbreak in 1921, those who had a sense of history would remember how God had worked before. We in these islands therefore should always pray for revival in the spirit of the psalmist's words:

'LORD, thou hast been favourable unto thy land...'
and the words of the hymn,
'Dear Shepherd of Thy chosen few,
Thy former mercies here renew...'

and again,

'O rend the heavens, come quickly down,
And make a thousand hearts Thine own!' [3]

The primacy of prayer

Much of Psalm 85 is a prayer:
Turn us, O God of our salvation, and cause thine anger towards us to cease. Wilt thou be angry with us for ever? Wilt thou draw out thine anger to all generations? (vv 4-5).

Believers must pray that God will 'turn' or restore them. The same Hebrew word translated 'turn' in verse 3, is translated 'restore' in Psalm 23 v. 3, 'He restoreth my soul'. Another verb which could be used is 'convert'. God's people are praying, 'Turn us, convert us, restore us from our backsliding.' The idea behind the expression, 'cause thine anger towards us to cease', is that of a cutting instrument which has its notches or teeth missing and is therefore rendered ineffective. The prayer is that God will make His anger and wrath against His wilful, rebellious people ineffective, and that He will revive them:

Wilt thou not revive us again that thy people may rejoice in thee? v. 6.

Robert Murray M'Cheyne, the Scottish preacher, rendered this cry for revival: 'Return and make us live anew.' He went on to say, 'It is the prayer of those who have received some life, but feel their need of more. They had been made alive by the Holy Spirit. They felt the sweetness and excellence of this new, hidden, divine life. They pant for more.' 4

God is sovereign in revival; it comes by his mercy, it is His work, but it is always preceded by fervent prayer. Every revival has been prepared for beforehand, as God has stirred His people to pray for it, and Lowestoft has been no exception either in 1860, 1870 or in 1921.

The Rev. Francis Cunningham, who was Vicar of Lowestoft from 1830 to within a few months of his death in 1863, was a man noted for his godliness and his prayerfulness. A Christian leader who had experience of revival in Lowestoft in 1860 and in 1921 was Dr. Eugene Stock of the Church Missionary Society; he recalled the earlier movement:

Prayer meetings were not common in the mid-nineteenth century in the Church of England, even among fervent evangelicals, certainly not for 'open' prayer. But I well remember the early Prayer Meeting at 7 a.m. on New Year's Day, in the funny old-fashioned school-room which would be quite filled. Very touching addresses were delivered and extempore prayers were offered by the vicar and curates and one layman, a leading local squire....When the memorable revival of 1859-60 occurred, Lowestoft was one of the places where there was special blessing....Mr. Cunningham died while the revival meetings were going on. 5

In the Baptist Church in 1870, the Rev. George Knight took up the weapon of prayer as soon as he arrived:

When he began his pastorate, a favourite phrase was prevalent in the prayer meetings, 'Help us O Lord, for we are brought werry low.' But after a few months this phrase dropped out of the prayer vocabulary, and praise above praise rose to the Throne of God's Grace.

Cottage prayer meetings were held in various parts of the town, and wherever a prayer meeting was held, some member of the family was converted to God. [6]

A great volume of prayer was made for revival in Lowestoft after the First World War. The town had survived a German bombardment; there was considerable unemployment involving many war veterans; the majority of Town Councillors, together with the editor of the *Lowestoft Journal*, scorned the proposal of a Christian councillor to seek the help of God in the conduct of local affairs. The Baptist Minister and the Vicar of Christ Church covenanted to pray that God would work. In the Baptist Church school-room eighty or ninety people met for prayer on Monday evenings, (including Bank Holidays), and for two years the regular church prayer meeting was almost entirely devoted to revival. 'What prayer meetings we used to have!' recalled one lady, referring to those meetings on Mondays at the Baptist Church and Saturday evenings at St. John's Parish Hall.

There is no more important preparation for revival than prayer, but however fervent it may be, it does not guarantee revival which comes by the sovereign power of God. At the same time there is no doubt that prayerless Christians and prayerless churches will not be revived.

THE RESULTS OF REVIVAL:

Revival is God's work within and upon Christians and churches and results are seen in the lives of believers, in the witness and work of churches and in the local community. Indicated in this psalm of revival are: the remembrance of it; the heart-cry for it and some of the results which flow from it:

God's People Rejoice

Wilt thou not revive us again that thy people may rejoice in thee? (v. 6).

Sorrow is turned into joy and weeping gives place to rejoicing when God moves in revival. It is the joy of salvation. The forgiveness of sins, the mercy of God and the cleansing power of the blood of Christ made the Christians and converts of Lowestoft rejoice and sing in 1921. 'O the singing!' people have said again and again as they tried to describe how the sound flooded out of the churches and into the streets. In the autumn the Scottish fishermen were set singing at Lowestoft and Yarmouth, in the churches and mission halls, in the open air, in their boats out on the fishing grounds and as they returned to their home ports with salvation in their souls.

The Word of God is Preached

I will hear what God the LORD will speak: for he will speak peace unto his people, and to his saints: but let them not turn again to folly.

Surely his salvation is nigh them that fear him; that glory may dwell in the land.

Mercy and truth are met together; righteousness and peace have kissed each other. (vv 8-10).

These words immediately follow prayer in the psalm and show that those who cry to God must be willing to hear what He has to say to them. The revival of 1921 fits into this Biblical pattern because, after prayer, preaching was central to it. Douglas Brown, Jock Troup and WP Nicholson were united in utterly rejecting the liberal theology, which was undermining the basic truths of man's ruin in sin, and salvation only through faith in the Lord Jesus Christ and his death and resurrection. Although the three men were very different in the style and manner of their preaching, they were impassioned preachers of the same Gospel, and God used them mightily. Douglas Brown may not always have been a careful expositor of Scripture but he believed the Bible fully and it was the source book of all his preaching.

The Second Advent was the main subject of the afternoon Bible Readings at Lowestoft, which were directed chiefly at Christians. Douglas Brown held a pre-millennial view of the Lord's return and was associated with the Advent Testimony and Preparation Movement. His views on the subject were well known to Montague Micklewright, a previous member of his church at Balham, who also heard the afternoon Bible Readings at Lowestoft. He commented that Douglas Brown emphasised 'the Judgement Seat of Christ and the response of believers to it'. So powerful were these studies that some people who were officers, teachers and members of local churches, were convicted of their hitherto false professions and truly converted. It was also said that church members put their communion cards in the collection bags and later asked for them back when they had been converted. Instead of turning again to the 'folly' of sin, backsliding and worldliness, many re-dedicated themselves to Christ and began to pursue holiness of life.

The Cross, and the blood of Christ as the only means of salvation, were central wherever the Gospel was preached in the revivals of 1921. It was at the Cross where the Lord Jesus Christ died for man's redemption that 'mercy and truth met together'and 'righteousness and peace kissed each other'.

O trysting place, where Heaven's love
And Heaven's justice meet! 7

Douglas Brown constantly pointed his hearers to Calvary—often with tears. No doubt there are those who would say that he was not sufficiently 'reformed' in his doctrinal position. He was the son of Archibald G, perhaps the best known of all Spurgeon's preachers, and he always said that he owed everything to his father. Montague Micklewright recalled, 'With regard to Arminianism and Calvinism, there was little awareness of the distinction in this country at that time. Douglas Brown was pre-eminently an evangelist; however, in balance with this it should be remembered that he was the successful and effective pastor of a thriving London church for over thirty years.' Dr. D M Lloyd-Jones warned evangelical Christians against thinking in terms of labels and parties, 'not realising that God often displays His sovereignty in this way, that though a man may be muddled in his thinking, as John Wesley was at certain points, God may nevertheless bless him and use him.' 8

Souls are saved in large numbers
The psalmist prays,
Show us thy mercy, O LORD, and grant us thy salvation. (v.7)
He then affirms,
Surely his salvation is nigh them that fear him...(v.9)
Wherever and whenever the Church of Christ has been revived, souls have been saved and added to it. So it was in Lowestoft, East Anglia, North-east

Scotland and Ulster in 1921. Wherever Douglas Brown, Jock Troup and WP Nicholson preached, people responded spontaneously to the gospel and hundreds of souls were saved without any modern evangelistic techniques. In Lowestoft on Wednesday, 9th March 1921, Douglas Brown gave the simplest of invitations and people immediately flooded into the aisles of the church. A steady stream of converts followed in subsequent weeks and months.

Robert Murray M'Cheyne said of revival:

Many flock to Christ. Who are these that fly like a cloud, and like doves to their windows? 'To him shall the gathering of the people be.' Just as all the creatures came into the ark, so poor sinners run in such a time. Laying aside their garments (Mark 10 v 50), their jealousies, they flee together into the ark Jesus. Oh, there is not a lovelier sight in all this world.

Souls are saved. 'Is not this a brand plucked out of the fire?' 'There is therefore now no condemnation to them which are in Christ Jesus. They are passed from death unto life.'

There is an awakening of fresh sinners. It is a sad state of things when sinners are bold in sin. It is an awful sign when sinners can live in sin, and yet sit unmoved under the preaching of the Word, cast off fear, and restrain prayer before God. But if the Lord were pleased to revive us again, this state of things would be changed. [9]

The Presence of God is Felt

Surely his salvation is nigh them that fear him; that
glory may dwell in our land. (v. 9)

CH Spurgeon commented on this verse: 'By His coming salvation is brought near, and glory, even the glory of the presence of the Lord, tabernacles among men.' [10] Revival has an atmosphere that can be felt; and the presence of God comes down, it is very real, and 'glory' dwells in the land. There was a great awareness of the presence of God in the Scottish Hebrides in 1949:

'The Rev. Duncan Campbell described revival as 'a community saturated with God'.

The presence of God was a universal, inescapable fact: at home, in the church, and by the roadside. Many who visited Lewis during this period became vividly conscious of the spiritual atmosphere before they reached the island.'[11]

There was an electric atmosphere in the packed Baptist Church in Lowestoft before there was any response to the Gospel. There was the father kneeling on the pavement outside the Fishermen's Bethel while his sons were being counselled; there was the man hanging over the railings of the harbour bridge in anguish of soul, and yet another pacing the sea front outside the hotel where Douglas Brown was having breakfast. A lad who was walking the two miles back to Oulton Broad after a meeting saw one or two kneeling by the path. 'Is this revival?' the believers in Oulton began to ask. Soon there were unprecedented scenes at the parish church of St. Michael. There was a sense of God's presence in the town and district. People came to see what God was doing, and at the September Convention Douglas Brown said that during the past months they had known the 'felt presence of Christ'.

An awesome awareness of God accompanied the preaching of Jock Troup at Yarmouth during the herring season. God came down into the market place after the stalls had closed and strong fishermen fell to the ground under conviction of sin, while others knelt in the street in the rain. Fisher-girls were similarly affected and unable to work in the curing yards until they were right with God; and men were saved out on the sea, miles from the preaching. When Jock left Yarmouth for Fraserburgh in the middle of the fishing season, the powerful presence of God went with him, and so it was when the fishermen returned to their home ports later.

The community is affected

Truth shall spring out of the earth; and righteous-ness shall look down from heaven. Yea, the LORD shall give that which is good; and our land shall yield her increase. Righteousness shall go before him; and shall set us in the way of his steps. (vv 11-13)

When there is spiritual awakening in a community, truth springs up among the people as though it grew out of the earth, and God, whose justice was satisfied at Calvary, looks down upon men with a smiling countenance. He is the giver of all spiritual and temporal blessings and He causes people to walk in righteous ways.

Revival has changed the face of communities, as it did in Wales in 1904 when it emptied public houses, filled chapels and inspired prayer meetings down the coal mines. It always has an effect upon the spiritual, moral and social life of the community.

In Lowestoft in 1921, the revival calmed the social unrest that seemed ready to boil over in the economic depression, when unemployment was so widespread, following the First World War. For many years it had the reputation of being a quiet town, especially on Sundays when there was a strong gospel witness in the churches, assemblies and missions which had participated in the revival. A succession of teams of open-air preachers would visit the town in the summer. When the Scottish fisher-folk returned each autumn, the friendships of revival days were renewed and, as voices blended in singing the songs of redemption, the atmosphere of the revival was in the air again.

Another notable and enduring result of the revival in Lowestoft was true Christian unity. The Baptist minister, three Anglican clergymen, the Port Missionary, a Primitive Methodist layman and Town Councillor, and the Salvation Army Officer experienced remarkable oneness in the work of proclaiming the Gospel of salvation in Christ alone. Henry Martin, the Rector of Oulton wrote:

'There was a happy spirit and unity realised between evangelical churchmen and the Baptist Church. Mr. Brown remarked to the writer that there were few towns where there would be found a Baptist minister and four evangelical clergy so absolutely one on the great fundamentals of the Faith, the inspiration of Scripture and the hope of glory of the Lord's return.' [12]

This unity in the Gospel and healthy interest in the Second Coming of Christ, continued for many years and became extremely strong again after the Second World War—thirty years after the revival!

Thomas Charles, who saw revival in Bala, North Wales, in 1791, said:

'Unless we are favoured with frequent revivals, and strong and powerful works of the Spirit of God, we shall in a great degree degenerate and have only a name to live; religion will soon lose its vigour, the ministry will hardly retain its lustre and glory, and iniquity in consequence will abound.' [13]

Eighty years have passed since we in England were favoured with a spiritual awakening, and it ended before it became nationwide.

Taking the town of Lowestoft as a typical example, we can see the enormity of the need. Godlessness and sin abound; vandalism, burglary, drunkenness and drugs are serious problems; the annual carnival is held on a Sunday, and throughout the summer an American Theme Park is crowded every Lord's Day. Over against this situation, how does the evangelical community in Lowestoft today compare with its 1921 predecessor? Henry Martin, Rector of Oulton, wrote in the *Churchman's Magazine*: 'There has been a distinct separation from the world and a stand made for God's day and Word made in the churches that participated in the revival outbreak.' Such an attitude is regarded as old-fashioned in many quarters today. There is still some clear, fervent gospel preaching in the town, but it is not as prominent as it was in the days of revival. Unity in the Gospel does still exist among churches and missions which stand apart from the modern ecumenical movement, but there is not much expression of it and the evangelical community is rather fragmented.

We desperately need another movement of the Holy Spirit, not only in Lowestoft but throughout the land. Scripture promises revival, abounds with examples of it as God's people turn back to Him in times of declension, and exhorts us to pray for it.

'Wilt Thou not revive us again.....?'

A hymn by RD Browne

(who was converted at Lowestoft on Wednesday, March 9th 1921)

Thou, Lord, hast given Thyself for our healing;
Poured out Thy life that our souls might be freed.
Love, from the heart of the Father, revealing
Light for our darkness and grace for our need.

Saviour of men, our humanity sharing
Give us a passion for souls that are lost.
Help us to follow, Thy gospel declaring;
Daily to serve Thee and count not the cost.

Pray we for men who today in their blindness
Wander from Thee and Thy kingdom of truth:
Grant them a sight of Thy great loving-kindness,
Lord of their manhood and guide of their youth.

Come, Holy Spirit, to cleanse and renew us:
Purge us from evil and fill us with power:
Thus shall the waters of healing flow through us;
So shall revival be born in this hour.

Give to Thy Church, as she tells forth the story,
Strength for her weakness and trust for her fears;
Make her a channel of grace for Thy glory,
Answer her prayers in the midst of the years.

Remembrances of 1921

God, by His wondrous grace throughout the years,
Visits His people with a new-found power—
And in that solemn and reviving hour
Strengthens their faith and banishes their fears.

So, in this eastern corner of our land,
His Spirit came in unexpected ways,
Leading both young and old to prayer and praise;
Downcast were raised and weaklings made to stand.

The Word was heard, and men discovered peace,
And freedom came to men who were enslaved,
The lost were found and sinners then were saved,
And saints rejoiced to see a large increase.

As from the sea the landward breezes blew,
Bringing a healthful burden in the train,
So may His Spirit come to us again,
So may His blessing come to us anew.

And so we pray, 'Revive Thy work, O Lord,
And bring to pass a glorious victory,
That multitudes may find their faith in Thee,
And prove the promise of Thy gracious Word.'

Robert D Browne.
(Written in 1989)

28 The woman then left her waterpot, and went her way into the city, and saith to the men, 29 Come, see a man, which told me all things that ever I did: is not this the Chrīst?

The left water-pot

A sermon preached by Douglas Brown at Lowestoft in 1921

'The woman then left her water-pot, and went her way into the city, and saith to the men, Come, see a Man which told me all things that ever I did: is not this the Christ?'
(John 4:28-29)

There are people who have a strange habit of leaving things behind. It is surprising, for instance, what a varied collection of articles are left behind in the house of God in the course of a year. It is very often a matter of sheer carelessness. But in the case of the Samaritan woman it is another kind of forgetfulness altogether. We cannot place it in the same category as that to which I have already referred. There is a gospel in the forgetfulness of this woman; there is something more than mere forgetfulness in this wonderful leaving behind.

The woman then left her water-pot. Why did she leave it behind? Because she had found something else, something that far transcended in value that old water-pot. If I were an artist I would paint this scene. The weary Christ sitting on Sychar's well. 'Jesus, therefore, being wearied with His journey.' What a comfort to us that that little detail has been recorded! It is one of the sentences in God's Word that brings Jesus Christ very near to us. He knew what it was to be tired. I am so glad that our wonderful Calvary Brother sat one afternoon on Sychar's well weary and worn, but, thank God! not sad. If I were an artist I would paint the scene, but I would paint the Saviour with a smile on His face as He looks towards the city watching someone as she trudges along the road, with her back towards Him and her face towards the town. She has peace in her soul and a message on her lips.

There was a sweeping victory for Jesus Christ that day. It was a case of sudden conversion. But there was something more wonderful still. Jesus Christ not only converted a human soul that afternooon, but He turned that Samaritan woman into a missionary. In that conversion there was the translation of a life out of darkness into light, a changing of the standards of life. Yes, the Divine Christ can take a life, and turn it in a new direction, and plant it in a new ministry, and inspire it with a new vision of the things that are worthy and high and true. Think of it! Jesus Christ did it all in one afternoon. That woman came to the well a prejudiced Samaritan; she left a believing Christian. She came a confirmed sinner; she left a contrite and believing soul. She came absolutely absorbed in temporal things; she left absolutely absorbed in eternal things.

Let us blot out from our minds for a moment the thought of the woman and the scene around, and let us look quietly at that left water-pot, for it has a message. It is a wonderful piece of pottery in the hands of the Spirit of God. What led up to her leaving that water-pot? It was something more than mere forgetfulness: there was a history at the back of that action. A great experience had been passed through; a life had been changed; old things had become new. It was all so wonderful and mysterious that the Samaritan woman was unable to tell the men of the city what had happened in her own soul; she could only proclaim Him as the Christ of God. There are people to-day who cannot explain that great and mighty power which changed their lives and translated them into the Kingdom of God's dear Son. The power that converts us, keeps us in His fellowship and companionship, is a power that we cannot explain or describe in so many words. The power that saves and sanctifies us is indescribable.

The left water-pot! Look at it. When that Samaritan woman started from the city that water-pot was everything to her. There was a whole life at the back of it. It was the one cause of her journey. Remember, too, the time of the day that she came to the well to draw water; sin does not like company in daylight. If you had told that woman that she would have left her water-pot behind, she would not have believed you. Yet it happened. She did leave it behind. And that woman is not the only one who has left behind what brought them out. Jesus Christ is the wonderful Prince of Peace, and He has a mystical way of breaking into the deepest darkness of a human life and sweetly leading it out into the sunshine of the love of God. When that woman left home, Jesus was nothing to her; the jar was everything. But as Jesus talked to her the positions were reversed; and when she made her way back to the city the jar was nothing to her—she left it behind—and Jesus was everything. That is not a theology; that is a theophany. It was a revelation of God in Christ which gave to that human soul a sublime forgetfulness of the things that hindered and spoiled life.

'*The woman then left her water-pot.*' How did the change take place? What was the method of the change? Christ makes His first intrusion into that life by means of a surprise. 'Then saith the woman of Samaria unto Him, How is it that Thou, being a Jew, askest drink of me, which am a woman of Samaria? for the Jews have no dealings with the Samaritans.' Jesus surprises her; He makes her think.

In the North of England a short time ago, during a series of services that I was conducting there, a man, who had no intention of attending any of the meetings, somehow or other found himself swept in with the crowd that filled the parish church. People were very surprised to see him in the house of God, for he was known to be a very ungodly man. Nobody spoke to him, but he went out of the church that night a new creation in Christ Jesus. He made a clean sweep of his drinking and betting. I prayed with him the following day, and I asked him what it was that had helped him to make the great decision. He said, 'While you were preaching about Calvary I understood for the first time that Jesus Christ loved me; and the thought of it was more than I could bear. I could not deny the fact of His love, for it was driven home to me by the impact of a great power from on high; but I knew I did not deserve it.' Yes, Jesus Christ surprises souls. Let us humbly thank God that His well-beloved Son, who died for us, but who is now enthroned in glory, speaks the word of power by His Holy Spirit that brings sinners into the realm of surprise.

See how Christ deals with this Samaritan woman. What was the next step? 'The woman saith unto Him, Sir, Thou hast nothing to draw with, and the well is deep: from whence then hast Thou living water?' She practically said to Christ, You are attempting to do the impossible. You offer me something, but I cannot see how you are going to give me what you offer. Is it not so to-day? Jesus Christ speaks to men and women concerning salvation; He speaks to them about eternal life. He speaks of that new consciousness of God that enters every department of the personality and brings a joy and satisfaction that can never pass away. But it all seems so impossible to them; and they say as the woman said, 'Thou hast nothing to draw with, and the well is deep: from whence then hast Thou that living water?'

Then Jesus Christ sweeps away all questioning and doubt, and there is born within her an earnest desire to receive all that God has to give in Jesus Christ. 'The woman saith unto Him, Sir, give me this water, that I thirst not.' In His ineffable grace and illimitable love God brings us to the place of surprise, and then shows us the impossible things; and as we look into His face we realize that all things are possible to Him if only we will trust Him. The Calvary Christ sweeps away all questioning and doubt, and there is left only one thing to do, and that is to give Him back the life we owe.

But with the awakening of that desire in her heart there comes the sense of sin. 'The woman saith unto Him, Sir, I perceive that Thou art a prophet. You know all about me; you know all about my past. All those things that shame me are known to you. Yet you have manifested love, with all my sin in the background.' 'Where sin abounded, grace did much more abound.' Jesus is leading her on. It will not be long before that water-pot will be left behind and she will be pressing on toward the town. Yes, and the work was done. The water-pot was left. The woman became a new creation in Christ Jesus. Back she goes to the town, a sinner saved by grace and converted into a home missionary, to tell the men of the town that she has discovered the Messiah; and the authority of her assertion lies buried deep in a real experience that nothing can eradicate. Jesus did it all in one afternoon.

In my father's Bible (a treasure that is of priceless value to me) I came across this question written against this passage: Why did she leave her water-pot behind? And underneath the question there were several suggestions. First, perhaps it was because she forgot it. Yes, eternal things had pushed out earthly things. She counted all things but loss for the excellency of the knowledge of Christ Jesus her Lord. When she was redeemed she forgot the things that were behind. That is what happens at Calvary. When you are brought to the foot of the Cross and you see the inner meaning of salvation in that great Sacrifice, you look up to Him in adoring love and you say, 'He saved others; Himself He could not save. He forgot Himself because He remembered me. Out of His weariness I gain my rest. Out of His agony I gain my peace. Out of His death I gain my life. Out of that unspeakable loneliness of Gethsemane and Calvary I gain my fellowship with the Father and with Jesus Christ. I discover that in His sweet redemptive forgetfulness for my sake He left everything behind.' Though He was equal with God, He made Himself of no reputation, but took upon Himself the form of a bond-slave, and became obedient unto death, even the death of the Cross.' And with the leaving of the water-pot behind you go into the city to proclaim the new vision of life everlasting in an eternal Christ.

Why did she leave her water-pot? I find that the second suggestion that my father gives in the margin of his Bible is this: That she might go the more quickly to tell the others. Maybe if she had carried the water-pot on her shoulder it would have taken her twenty minutes longer to reach the village. 'Seeing we also are compassed about with so great a cloud of witnesses, let us lay aside every weight, and the sin which doth so easily beset us.' Therefore she left the burden behind; she left behind that which might have hindered her progress; she left behind that which might have fettered her in her witness. She left her water-pot behind because she had met the King and had received the King's benediction, and she had to be away on the King's business, which required haste, and, therefore, anything that was an impediment to her witness had to be left behind. The woman left her water-pot in order that she might run the more quickly to tell the others about Christ. We all have our water-pot, but it is not the same in any two cases. It may be pride. It may be an inordinate desire to keep up our position and reputation. Or it may be that we are so anxious about our reputation that we fear being misunderstood even by our best friends. Oh, to be so fascinated by Jesus Christ that the idea of sacrifice may never enter the region of our thoughts because the love of Christ constrains us! Is there a water-pot that we ought to leave behind? May His power so fall upon our hearts and lives that we may be made swifter messengers of His eternal truth. If there is in the realm of our Christian witness anything which, by being left behind, would help us to run the more swiftly to do the King's business, then may God make us willing in the day of His power.

The third suggestion that my father makes as to why she left the water-pot behind is this: Perhaps she left it for Christ's own use. You see, He was weary and thirsty, and He had done so much for her, and she loved Him, but she felt she was unworthy to tell Him so. She wanted to say a good deal, but somehow she could not say it. She wanted to do something tangible to prove her gratitude for all that He had done for her, but somehow she had not the courage to say a word. But love has a way of expressing itself. She left the water-pot behind; and, maybe, she said to herself, I hope He will use it. It belongs to me, but if only those hands of His may lift up that belonging of mine and make some use of it, it will be the highest honour that He can ever bestow upon this life which He has redeemed. Is there something in your life that you feel could be of service to Him? You may feel that you are unworthy to offer it to Him, but leave it behind, and then make your way along the pathway of duty and witness, and let the great Calvary surprise so fill your soul that men may know that you have come face to face with the Christ who has fathomed the deepest depths of your heart and who has brought life and immortality to light through the Gospel. The very thing that you leave behind He will use for His own refreshment.

Why did she leave her water-pot behind? My father makes still another suggestion: Did she leave it as a pledge that she was coming back again? That is more than likely. Perhaps she left something with Jesus that made it necessary for her to come back again. It was just as if she wanted to tell Him, and she told Him by means of a piece of earthenware, how much He had done for her. It was just as if she wanted to tell Him that it had not been just a passing emotion, that it was not just a superficial thing that had happened in her heart and life. I think the woman wanted Jesus to know that she was coming back for more. Just as we are dependent upon Him for the giving of life, so we are dependent upon Him every day for the sustenance of that life which He has imparted to us.

There is one other suggestion in the margin of my father's Bible. Did it mean that the convert had become a missionary? When Jesus Christ that day emancipated her from the thraldom of her old life and led her into the liberty of the Gospel, the standards of life were altered for her. She realized that she had been saved to serve. May we not read on her water-pot these words: 'Divine Master, the elixir of life to me will be to bring others to Thee'?

That is the simple story of the left water-pot. What is the application to our own hearts and lives? This place has been Sychar's well. Jesus Christ has been here quietly drawing and pleading. Perhaps no spiritual purpose brought you here, but He has met you. Life for you can never be the same again. I had a day-dream. This service was over. The clock was striking the midnight hour as I made my way back into this building. It was empty, as I thought, and dark; but as I entered I heard the sound of the rustling of angels' wings, and I wondered what they were doing. And I went up to one of the angels, and I saw that he was writing a record, and he said to me, 'Don't you see, preacher, there is a water-pot, and there is another, and there is another? I am writing the history of these left water-pots, and these records will be taken back to Heaven because there is joy among the angels of God over sinners repenting.' If there is a water-pot that Christ would have you leave behind, may He give you His Calvary grace, that you may be more than conqueror through Christ who loves you.

Our records and God's remedy

A sermon preached by Jock Troup

The message I have to give you here is a message for those who perhaps do not know the Lord Jesus Christ yet. Although it may be a little stern, I ask you just to wait patiently, because the portion of the message that may be stern may rouse something in you. I trust to God it will, because I always feel this, that when the Lord hurts, He hurts for the purpose of healing.

So if you turn to the book of Job, chapter 16, and verse 19, you will read these words: 'Behold, my witness is in heaven, and my record is on high.' In Psalm 144, verse 3 'Lord, what is man, that Thou takest knowledge of him! or the son of man, that Thou makest account of him!' —or, as it should be expressed more correctly, 'that Thou shouldst make a record of him.' In Romans 14, verse 12: 'So then every one of you shall give account of himself to God.' In 1 Peter 4, verse 5: 'Who shall give account to Him that is ready to judge the quick and the dead.' If I were to give a title to my message to-night, it would be 'OUR RECORDS AND GOD'S REMEDY'. We have all that is necessary in the Word of God to reveal to us the meaning of our records, and also the wonderful redemption wrought out by Christ, the remedy for our records.

This is an absolute fact, that every man and every woman born into this world, from the day they were born they begin to make a record, and that record is recorded in high heaven. The Word of God makes that very clear and plain. Every individual man and woman, it does not matter who they are, it does not matter what family they have been brought up in, it matters not what influence they may have, it does not matter where they have been, or what they have seen, or what they have done—there is one thing God Almighty's Word makes clear and plain, that we are each one of us making a record. This is a fact. I believe it is an established fact in the realm of nature. I do not know whether you are aware of this or not, but any astronomer of any standing can give you a wonderfully accurate account of the life of any of the stars or planets that are in the heavens. I have read something of them by Sir James Jeans, and others. And it is really marvellous how much these men are able to tell you about these heavenly bodies. They have a record, and that record can be traced, and these men with the ability do trace the record of these heavenly bodies.

This is another fact. Any geologist of any worth or standing can make the rocks speak. We had a very little man in Scotland, but he was a big Christian, one of the biggest Christians that ever I met in my life. He was MP for one of the constituencies in Lanarkshire, named Robert Maclaren, a clever man—I do not think there is a part of the earth's surface where any mining has been done but that man visited it. That was his business. He was Mines Inspector in our own country, but he was also a geologist of no mean standing. Often I have walked with Robert Maclaren, and he could make the rocks speak. I didn't know the language. I did not have the ability to decipher what they were saying, but that man could tell you by looking at the strata of rock just exactly what the rock had passed through since its creation almost.

Then this also is an absolute fact, and I know that no man will gainsay me. The trees and the plants have their own record. Is it not a fact that the botanist can tell you? The trees have a language, and the botanist can make them unfold the record of their existence on the face of this earth. If these things which are inanimate and lifeless have a record, and an accurate record, and the man who has the ability can make them unfold their record, when you get a man who has life, and a quality of life and a kind of life beyond the plant life or any other type of life, do you mean to tell me that there is no record kept of that particular individual's life? Yet there are men and women who try to blink the fact. I tell you, we have a witness in heaven, and you and I have our record in God Almighty's recording house in heaven above.

A great many people think they can creep into the City of London and be lost here because there are about eight and a half million in the great mass. I want to tell you, I care not whether it is the mightiest city we have in the British Empire, or in the world, or the tiniest hamlet there is on some hillside, we have reached the stage in our civilization when every man and every woman, every boy and every girl, whether we believe it or not, the Authorities have come to the place where they keep a record of our movements. Some people have tried to make themselves believe they can move out of the realm of the influence of the Authorities. The man who thinks so is living in a fool's Paradise.

This was something that was known to the ancients, too. Any of you acquainted with the Book of Ezra will remember how, after the return from the captivity and the commencement of the building of the walls of the city of Jerusalem, those enemies of God's people tried to frustrate the plan of the rebuilding of the city of Jerusalem and its walls, and you will remember the attitude they took up. First of all, they tried to frighten them. Secondly, they tried by the Fifth Columnist method. That is not new to Hitler or to anyone else of our modern civilisation. Fifth Columnist work has been the strategy of the Devil himself from the very commencement. If he cannot get you by fight, or by fright, he will get you by feint. So he tried to get them by feint. When these men here could not get at God's leaders at that time by fight, or by fright, and could not get round about them by feint, do you remember what they tried to do? Shimshai the scribe, and some of the other leaders of the people in the valley, wrote a letter to King Artaxerxes, and asked him to search the records of the great Persian Empire, and they would discover that these people who had come back and were rebuilding the city wall at Jerusalem and seeking to reinstate the religion of Israel were bad people. Not only were they bad, but they had been troublesome in the earlier part of their history in Jerusalem. Isn't it a remarkable thing that these peoples of antiquity went to the bother not only of keeping a record of their own nation, but a record of the nations around them.

I want to tell you, I care not who you are, or where you have come from, if you read this wonderful Book here, you will discover that God Almighty has a record of that life of yours. There is not an incident, nor an accident, there is no part of your being but God day by day has a record of every movement. This is a very remarkable thing in modern science to-day. Any man or woman who has any knowledge of modern science knows that this is a fact. The human voice can be recorded on a simple wax disc, and not only can it be recorded, but it is beyond comprehension almost that on that wax disc, in spite of the fact that it is unseen, it is recorded and retained, and from that wax disc can be reproduced the very words that were spoken or sung. Is it not a marvellous thing? I remember when I came down to the City of London nearly twenty years ago. I was invited to come down to one of the Recording Companies here to make some gramophone records. I never knew I could sing. I know I have got plenty of volume, but for melody I don't know. However, they invited me down, and I was given the job of singing twenty four hymns. I can tell you I was exhausted after it was done. It was not an easy thing. After the records were made, the Company sent the test set right away back north to my wife. Some of the Canadian boys here know my family. Little Rona was only 1½ years old at the time. I was up in Aberdeen conducting a mission. My wife was proud that her husband had had the privilege of singing on a gramophone record, but we hadn't a gramophone of our own, so she had to go and borrow one from a neighbour. She gathered the neighbours in, and put the first record on the gramophone. Little Rona stood and looked at that thing; then her little breast began to heave, and she looked at it and started to cry, 'Oh! Daddy, will you no' come out?' It was so real to the child. She could not realize what was happening. She thought her Daddy was inside that little box. She had some imagination, didn't she? But isn't it a marvellous thing that the very words that I sang, and the mistakes as well, were faithfully recorded. I will tell you what one lady said about those records in Glasgow. She said, 'Well, he's no' a good singer, but he's earnest.'

If you read God's Word carefully, you will realize that every man and woman on God's earth is making a three-fold record. Get hold of this. I trust to God you will. Every one of your *words* is being recorded. I sometimes shudder to think of the horror and the blasphemy of the language that is being used by men to-day, not only against God but against His Christ. They forget, indeed they are ignorant of the fact that every idle word men speak they shall give an account thereof at the day of judgment. If you had any thought of eternity, if you had any thought of your soul's eternal welfare, it would shock you to the very foundation of your triple being to know that God has a record of your every word. Supposing I had some magic power to unfold on the platform the words that have been spoken by the men and women gathered here. Do you think you could face them? I tell you before God I could not face mine. My head would bow with shame.

But God has a record of our *works*. 'And I saw the dead, small and great, stand before God; and the books were opened: and another book was opened, which is the book of life: and the dead were judged out of those things which were written in the books, according to their works. And the sea gave up the dead which were in it; and death and hell delivered up the dead which were in them: and they were judged every man according to their works.' The books of works—do you think you could face them? I could not face mine. These hands of mine have done shameful things. I would not like it if God Almighty to-day would send an angel from heaven and reveal to other men and women what these hands have been guilty of. I believe it would put me insane. But that is not all.

The Word of God speaks of a record of our *thoughts*. Have you ever read: 'The Word of God is quick, and powerful, and sharper than any two-edged sword, piercing even to the dividing asunder of soul and spirit, and of the joints and marrow, and is a discerner of the thoughts and intents of the heart'? God records what you are thinking.

I do not know anybody I have ever met who would have the audacity to say that in word, in thought, and in deed, they have always done those things which have been well pleasing to God. I would tell them to their face they were a liar. 'If we say we have not sinned, we make Him a liar.' I wonder how many men to-day are afraid of their record.

God has a wonderful remedy for records. Do you know it? I am thinking of a fellow who came in to Tent Hall one night, bearing the same name as myself, John Troup. That fellow could drink. He was seldom sober. He wanted to see me. He claimed relationship. Well, the Devil is no relation to mine. We had an old sailor who used to be at the door. He was converted, but I think his temper would have been better to have been a little more tempered. He got into grips with Troup, and in a moment Jimmy Gray fell like a log on the floor. He was taken to hospital, but before he got there life had gone. Troup was arrested, and put in prison. I was asked to go up and make a statement, which I did, and which got him released from prison. Jimmy Gray was suffering from his heart, and he was an old man. When Troup got out from the gate of the prison there was a lady on the opposite side of the street, and he said to me afterwards, 'When I looked at that lady, and that lady looked at me, I heard something say to me, 'Yes, that's the fellow that murdered the man in Tent Hall.'" That fellow ran until he was exhausted. Every time he stopped his conscience smote him, and when I saw him that evening you could have lifted him with one hand, he was so exhausted, beat to the world.

I am going to tell you this. God Almighty has that three-fold record of yours. Do you know God's remedy for it?

Oh! why was He there as the Bearer of sin,
If on Jesus my guilt was not laid,
Oh! why from His side flowed the sin-cleansing blood,
If His dying my debt hath not paid?

He took my record to the Cross. That is the Gospel. The very fact that you are not only a debtor, but a double-dyed sinner: the very fact that that record has been kept from the very day of your birth to the present moment of time and you cannot do anything about it, there it is indelibly inscribed in the books of God in heaven—is the very reason why Jesus Christ intervened on your behalf and mine, to deal with our rotten record. And not only to deal with our record, but thank God, to give us the blessings of life. Without a mark on it, unmarred by sin, untainted, untouched, untarnished by anything that belongs to sin, God has given us a life in Christ. That is the new birth.

You see I was born, and I made a record until I was born again; and God Almighty took my old record, and in the blood of His Son He blotted it out. As a thick cloud He blotted out the writing that was against me, nailing it to His Cross. All my sins are gone. Glory be to God! They are gone for ever.

I remember I went to a little place called Portobello, not very far from Edinburgh. On the sands of Portobello there were literally thousands of people, walking the promenade, and on the steps. I remember how at the close of that day, what they call the Fair Monday, the people left; and I will never forget the sight they left behind them. They left litter that no Municipal Cleansing Department could have cleaned. Indeed, I would have defied any cleansing department to have done anything about it. But the following morning I was up and out on the promenade very early, and believe it or not, something like unto a miracle had taken place. There was not the hand of a man near it either. It was all done so silently and swiftly, and yet it was accomplished in such a mighty way that I would have defied any person to have found any litter or the trace of a footstep on that unbroken stretch of sand. Something had happened. The tide had gradually come in, sweeping everything before it; and then, when it receded, it took everything with it, leaving those sands just an unbroken stretch, as though the footprint of man had never been upon it. Let me tell you, that God Almighty has a remedy for your sin that can leave that life of yours cleaner than those Portobello sands. 'If we walk in the light as He is in the light, we have fellowship one with another, and the blood of Jesus Christ, His Son, cleanseth us from all sin.' I always wonder at that little word of three letters—ALL, all my words, all my works, all my thoughts.

Every one of them; they are all gone.

I want to ask you, do you know anything about God Almighty's remedy? I want to tell you that where you sit to-night, just as you are, without one plea, in a moment of time God can transform that life of yours. Do you know how He does it? By the blood of His Son, and by the regeneration of His blessed Holy Spirit. This is not the improvement of the old; this is not a reformation. This is God Almighty regenerating the soul of a man or a woman, not by giving them a new leaf, but by imparting a new life. Do you want to get rid of your record? *Here is the opportunity.*

Lowestoft, twenty five years after the revival

When she was thirteen, my mother was converted in the church where the revival occured, and was a member seven years before the Revival broke out. My father came to the church through the large bible classes that were held for both young men and women on Sunday afternoons. An apprentice carpenter and joiner, he was one of the early converts when the revival began. My parents were married in 1926 by Hugh Ferguson who was still the pastor.

I was converted in September 1946 and many of my generation agree with me that those post war years were the most spiritually fruitful there have been in Lowestoft since the revival. It is nearly eighty years since that revival took place, the last to occur in England and if there is to be another it must be the outpouring of the Spirit of God, as it has been with all the revivals in the history of the church. In the years immediately after the second war there were conditions in church life in Lowestoft that were similar to those before the revival of 1921. If there is to be another revival there must be a reformation in which at least those conditions return.

Prayer
When I was converted as a sixteen year old, I could not conscientiously ask the pastor to baptise me unless I was attending the prayer meeting. Nobody told me this, it was the whole spiritual atmosphere of the church—and I knew that it had been like that since 1921.

Bible study
From the beginning, I was taught to love the Bible and study it. There were men and women who set a splendid example in this. Most prominent among them was AB Cooper, a local dentist, and a deacon of the church. He had been converted in 1915 when Oswald Chambers came to Lowestoft. He was prominent in the revival, and it always seemed that his main purpose was to preach and teach the word of God.

Gospel preaching

This was a feature of churches and ministers in the town and continued for at least a decade.

FH Kingsbury had come to the Baptist Church as pastor during some of the worst days of the war and he was an evangelist. Lowestoft was the home port of the Mission Ship and the skipper obtained permission to take Frank Kingsbury up to Scapa Flow to preach to the officers and men of the Home Fleet. I can remember Sundays when Mr Kingsbury started the evening service in the church and then went along the street to Woolworth's bombed site and preached there. After the war, when people returned to the town on holiday he would have open air witness near the swing bridge after the Sunday evening service.

Henry Sutton came to Lowestoft as Vicar of Christ Church immediately after the war, and was a man with an evangelistic zeal who made a powerful impact. He later became the General Secretary of the South American Missionary Society.

Peter Street followed Henry Sutton at Christ Church and he used to set a pulpit on a bombed site in the High Street near Christ Church and preach the gospel.

George Backhouse, the Elim pastor ministered in the town throughout the war and as well as his faithful ministry he was in the fire service. Whenever there was an opportunity to preach in the open-air in those post-war years, he was there.

Stanley Pert was the Rector of St Michaels, Oulton and he and the people from Commodore Mission were eager to preach the gospel by Oulton Broad.

Open-air preaching went on each summer on the beach and promenade. A number of teams came each year such as the Faith Mission and Cliff College Trekkers, who were lead by Herbert Silverwood, a former miner. I have vivid memories of his warm sense of humour and his passionate pleading for souls on summer evenings on the sea front.

Ministers I have mentioned and some other church leaders displayed a unity in the Gospel that was similar to that of 1921. Lead by Henry Sutton and Stanley Pert a monthly meeting was arranged called Saturday Rendezvous. It was held in the Baptist Church, the preaching was both evangelistic and for Christians, it regularly attracted congregations of five hundred and was known in different parts of the country.

Frederick P Wood, founder of the national Young Life Campaign, who had been inspired by Douglas Brown in the 1920s preached in Lowestoft a number of times during this post war period.

Another important factor in church life in Lowestoft at this time was the return of the Scottish fisherfolk in the autumn. The spiritual life of the town would be lifted to a higher plane, mainly because all their boats would be tied up on Sundays and they would crowd churches, missions and assembles. I was greatly influenced as a young Christian and I know now that it was because many of these were revival men and women!

An annual convention for Christians was first held when Douglas Brown was in the town and still continues. The main reason why the convention and Saturday Rendezvous continued into the 1960s was the faithfulness and dedication of Edwin Barnes who followed Stanley Pert as Rector of Oulton.

Perhaps the greatest difference between those days that I can remember so clearly and the present, was the gospel preaching that went on consistently in so many congregations in the town and in the open air. I have tried to highlight three great needs of God's people now that we are so far from revival. We must return to these simple biblical practices:

Prayer, Love for the word of God, Gospel Preaching.

Wilt thou revive us again: that thy people may rejoice in thee? PSALM 85 V 6

References

CHAPTER 1.
1. From a sermon by A. Douglas Brown, printed in the *Christian Herald*, June 23rd, 1921.
2. *Keswick Week*, 1921.
3. Brown. *Revival Addresses*. Pub. Morgan and Scott 1922. Pages 80-83.
4. Brown. *The Great Harvester*. Pub. Stanley Martin 1923. The Dedication.

CHAPTER 2.
1. *Keswick Week*, 1921.
2. Ibid.
3. Ibid.
4. Ibid.
5. There were ministers and leaders in the town, who did not support the revival and, in some cases, opposed it. The Wesleyan minister, the Rev. Shiman Corlett was not in favour of his people attending the meetings. It was said that one of the leaders of a Strict Brethren Assembly stood on the pavement opposite the Baptist Church and counted his people as they went in!

CHAPTER 3.
1. *The Christian, June 2nd 1921.*
2. *The Churchman's Magazine*, 1921, page 177.

CHAPTER 4.
1. *The Christian*, June 2nd, 1921.
2. A char-a-banc was originally an open vehicle with seats, but later referred to a tourist coach.
3. *Keswick Week*, 1921.
4. *The Christian Herald*, June 30th, 1921.
5. *The Christian*, June 30th, 1921.
6. *The Christian Herald*, July 14th, 1921.
7. *The Christian*, July 21st, 1921.
8. *The Christian*, July 28th, 1921.

9. A maroon was a loud, explosive firework, often used as a warning.
10. *Norfolk News and Weekly Press*, Saturday Sept. 10th 1921.
11. From a sermon by Douglas Brown printed in the *Christian Herald*, October 13th, 1921.
12. *The Christian Herald*, December 1st, 1921.
13. From a sermon by Douglas Brown printed in *The Christian Herald*, December 1st, 1921.

CHAPTER 5.
1. Stewart. *Our Beloved Jock*. Pub. Revival Literature 1964. Pages 6-7.
2. *Yarmouth and Gorleston Times*. Quoted in *The Christian Herald*, November 24th, 1921.
3. *The Christian Herald*, December 1st, 1921.
4. Ibid.

CHAPTER 6.
1. Char-a-banc, see reference 2, Chapter 4.
2. Ritchie. *Floods upon the Dry Ground*. Pub. Peterhead Offset 1983. Page 98.
3. Stewart. *Our Beloved Jock*. Pub. Revival Literature 1964. Page 11.
4. Ritchie. *Floods upon the Dry Ground*. Pub. Peterhead Offset 1983. Page 52.
5. *The Railway Signal*, the magazine of the Railway Mission, quoted in *Floods upon the Dry Ground. Page 108*.
6. Ibid. Page 14. Quoted from *The People's Journal, December 17th 1921*.
7. Slater. *A Sea-faring Saga*. Page 41.
8. *The Christian Herald*, January 12th 1922.
9. Stewart. *Our Beloved Jock*. Pub. Revival Literature 1964. Page 15. Quoted from *The People's Journal*, December 17th, 1921.

CHAPTER 7.
1. Brown. *Revival Addresses*. Pub. Morgan and Scott 1922. Pages 19-20.
2. Stewart. *Our Beloved Jock*. Pub. Revival Literature 1964. Page 19.
3. Ibid. Foreword.
4. Ibid. Pages 4-5.

References

5. Ibid. Page 24.
6. Orr. *Revival and Evangelism in Britain*, 1920-1940. Unpublished. Page 8.

CHAPTER 8.
1. Lazell. *From the Forest I Came*. Pub.Concordia. Page 154.
2. Peckham. *Heritage of Revival*. Pub. The Faith Mission. Page 50.
3. Orr. *Revival and Evangelism in Britain*, 1920-1940. Unpublished. Page 18.
4. Evans. *The Welsh Revival of 1904*. Pub. Evangelical Press of Wales 1969. Page 166.
5. *The Christian*, May 26th, 1921.
6. *The Christian*, June 9th, 1921.

CHAPTER 9
1. *The Revival*, May 11th, 1861. Reference was made in this report to the *East Suffolk Mercury*.
2. *The Revival*, June 22nd, 1861.
3. William Cowper, 1731-1800.
4. *The Cry for Revival*, sermon by R Murray M'Cheyne, Crusade Reprint, 1959.
5. Eugene Scott DCL *The Christian*, June 16th, 1921.
6. *Centenary Souvenir of the London Road Baptist Church, Lowestoft*. Pub. Rogers 1913. Page 47.
7. Elizabeth Celphane, 1830-1869.
8. Lloyd-Jones. *The Puritans, Their Origins and Successors*. Banner of Truth Trust 1987. Page 10.
9. *The Cry for Revival*, sermon by R Murray M'Cheyne, Crusade Reprint, 1959.
10. Spurgeon. *Treasury of David*, Psalm 85:9.
11. Woolsey. *Duncan Campbell*. Pub. Hodder and Stoughton 1974. Page 121.
12. *The Churchman's Magazine*, 1921. Page 176.
13. Evans. *Revivals, Their Rise, Progress and Achievements*. Pub. Evangelical Press of Wales. Page 32.

APPENDIX 1.
The Great Harvester, a sermon by Rev. A. Douglas Brown. Pub. Stanley Martin. Page 37.

APPENDIX 2.
Our Records and God's Remedy, a sermon by Jock Troup, quoted in *Our Beloved Jock*, by Dr. James Alexander Stewart. Pub. Revival Literature 1964. Page 24.